G000153341

LIFE GOES ON

Alex Kahney

LIFE GOES ON

"Who cares what fools say"

"The reason that books are not censored is the censors don't read them"

For Joe Zanghi

Prologue

Today, April 4, 2020, is the ten-year anniversary since I lost my two beautiful daughters, eight-year-old Selene Frances and six-year-old Cale Frances, to abduction by their Japanese mother in Tokyo. As I write, my house I once purchased in Denenchofu—a florid suburb laid out loosely based on the garden city design of Welwyn in Hertfordshire, England, transposed to the banks of the Tama river lazing through Kanagawa—is being repossessed and auctioned off by my Japanese mortgage lenders. I'm reminded that I lost everything in Japan. And with that, a half my life.

I'm also reminded that I have something to set down. My previous book *Life & Nihonjin* (published 2011) describes my experiences of Japanese child abduction from the ground at that time. Written as it was still unfolding, the story was unresolved. Since then, people have asked me what happened to your children in the end? Did you regain contact with them? The present book describes what followed next: *Life Goes On.*

Three years after my children's abduction, while I was staying as a temporary houseguest with my Mom and brothers in San Francisco, I accepted a job as a writer of medical communications in Richmond near London. So I returned to U.K. after a twelve-year absence. I landed at Heathrow airport carrying an inordinately heavy handheld duffel bag of clothes with no credit card and only £5 in cash—a banknote my Mom dug up that morning before I set off, and put in my pocket. It was not enough to cover the train fare from the airport to Richmond. I'd been away from England so long I had not reckoned the price increases of tickets on London's Tube—or of anything else. I walked sixteen kilometers alongside a blaring M4 motorway to my new residence, carrying my weighty load. A penniless prodigal son. What was I thinking as I hefted that burden? I had two main aims: to seek redress for my daughters using what help I could recruit in U.K., and to rebuild my life back in my native country. What does rebuilding a life from nothing but a bag of clothes involve, and what did I find in England? *Life Goes On*.

Life Goes On follows roughly the format of, and is a companion volume and follow-up to, *Life & Nihonjin*. The present book, like its predecessor, contains a selection of e-mail missives, anecdotes, and conjectures I wrote to long-standing friends, reproduced chronologically*, between 2012 and the present (2020). They are a record of my experiences trying to rebuild a life in England during that time. A lot of the e-mails were tapped on my phone as what they report was happening, lending them an immediacy. Interspersed between a few of the e-mails are replies from my correspondents *in italics*, inserted where necessary for context. Unlike in *Life & Nihonjin*, for this book I have not disguised anyone's proper names.

A universal piece of feedback I received from readers of *Life & Nihonjin* was "I like the unusual e-mail format, but I don't think anyone else would!" Everyone said the same. My excuse for compiling this book of e-mails is, what's the difference between a book of e-mails and a book of letters? There have been many anthologies of authors' old correspondences. This book is a record of recent times and a personal memoir. To quote Robert Graves in the Prologue to his memoir, *Goodbye to All That*: "If any passage still gives offence after all these years, I hope to be forgiven."

Richmond, Surrey, 2020   A.K.

---

*Entries are presented numbered in order of composition, although the numbers have no further intrinsic meaning.

Acknowledgments

For making this book possible: deepest thanks to my wife Natasha and to my mate Adrian Roots.

San Francisco, October 2012

1

Damn, I was sitting in Biergarten in beautiful evening weather yesterday when a leaf spirit fell onto my book I was reading. This brown, dry, curled leaf was the shape of a gnome face, with a mouth, nose, and two round cut-out eyes. When I held up the leaf against any backdrop, the eyes appeared to move around. It was a human-like spirit of some sort. And it fell on my book looking at me. Like an idiot I put it in my bag, and this morning it was all ground up into crumbs. I didn't even take its picture on my camera! Did it make me forget to do so?

A while ago this happened, and I do have a pic somewhere. I looked up and saw an Egyptian High Priest in a cloud! This was one of the cloud faces I have witnessed many times over the years, a perfect example. A perfect example of a cloud face is absolute verisimilitude, statuesque reproduction of human or animal form, not a mere resemblance if you look hard, but a solid representation of a being made of cloud. An unmistakable being, in the sky! I reached for my phone camera and guess what—the shutter "button" (circle to tap on the screen) was missing! I couldn't take the pic. I fiddled with the camera and finally got the shutter button to take the pic—but by then the form had mostly changed shape and was nearly gone. Let me find the pic I took....

2

On Paul Auster's latest book (impression so far): I think that music composers— I'm talking about pop music composers such as Paul McCartney etc.—which is the only music I know really—have in them only a limited number of melodies. By limited, I mean that the number of inspired melodies is finite, not that it is necessarily a small number. I might even dare to say that the number is not only quite large, but also that it is more-or-less the same for every composer. These are two hypotheses that you will surely not have heard before, I bet! I think that pop music composers (songwriters) have roughly one hundred good ditties in them, after which they become repetitive and lose their better ability—mainly probably because they themselves can feel their power declining. Yes, the number one hundred is about the figure I reached when I wrote all my songs. The same consideration also applies (otherwise I could not think it was a general rule) to my favorite songwriters (melodists), such as McCartney, Lennon, Brian Wilson, Mick Jones of The Clash—who also reached the number around one hundred then seem to have lost their craft. For my own part, I think that I tried lots of different tricks as a songwriter (for example going from major to minor, minor to major, major to seventh chord, and so on), as technical exercises, and now I feel that if I had to write new songs I don't have new ideas that I have not tried yet. So maybe I am exhausted as a songwriter, or if I wrote new songs they would sound like my previous songs and lack the sparkle of originality!

And here is what I think of Paul Auster today. I think he is a writer who has run out of things to say. His latest book is beautifully written and flows so nicely I have nearly finished it already, and certainly would have finished if I did not have to go to work today and yesterday—but so far I have not learned from the book any new wisdom or insights, not heard any secrets that the author wanted to tell. Auster seems to have run out of things to say, like a used-up pop composer.

3

Funny, Paul Auster wrote in his latest book that when he briefly moved to the San Francisco Bay Area (Seventies? early Eighties?) he couldn't settle and soon had to move back to New York. San Fran was not big enough for him. He wrote that he either had to reside in the biggest "most unliveable" city, if he were to live in a city at all, or else away from the city—such as in a French country village. I have felt this way as well. San Fran is too small for me. I have already done everything here. This city does not regenerate, or not fast enough to be constantly changing. I really would like to live in the countryside, away from all the crowds and noise, but I enjoy visiting the city, or staying there for short periods. Tokyo was the same. Even now I miss my little social world—the *gaijin* places I habituated. I knew all the *gaijin* hangouts but I had long since honed down the ones that suited me (i.e., the ones you and I frequented—Dickens, Black Lion, Aldgate, Hobgoblin Roppongi, Hobgoblin Shibuya, and my own personal local pub, O'Carolan's Jiyugaoka). I knew a world of *gaijin* bands, and playing [live] in certain places. During 2010 and '11, I was too depressed to think about those much. I also miss some other things about Tokyo—its crushing loneliness, its places screaming out for company. There are many pockets of Tokyo to where I returned constantly—the park and open space at Oi, looking out on the water, for example. And then there are the countless places where I left a memory. Tokyo is so bleak—all of Japan is bleak, bleakness is its character—borne by the many millions of people who lived silent, secretive lives there, all their spirits dwell in that vast city. There are places I remember, which I could probably never find again. Places I went to several times, such as faraway soccer grounds, but I cannot remember where they are, their names and whereabouts. Now, I could not find them. A vast maze of memories. So vast, a brain-sized maze. A map of the human brain.

The reason that the Fates prevented me from selling my house in Tokyo—even when I was almost prepared to give it away at a really low price—is that I shall have to return there to live one day. I will. And my girls will run up and down those stairs again, and burst in and out those rooms and sit warmly in that bath again. They will chase away the ghosts of that haunted house.

4

The Richard III "find" [skeleton discovered in Leicester, U.K.] seems like a load of nonsense to me. What do you think? The archeologists claim the skeleton was "unbound, just thrown in the grave." And yet it survived intact for over five hundred years. Nonsense alert. Also nice hunchback—just like Laurence Olivier's onstage (a cushion). With all news reports, we never hear any background details, so it's hard to "unearth" (pun) what led to the discovery. Usually a team of archeologists can carbon-date a skeleton. Not sure how the "modern-day living ancestors" of Richard III were tracked down and gave DNA samples that match those of the skeleton. This seems a nice example of a piece of claptrap that sounds scientific to the lay public and hence goes unquestioned.

A while ago (sometime in mid-twentieth century) the tomb of Henry III (I believe) was opened. This tomb was in Westminster Abbey and there's no doubt the remains deposited therein were the king's. The body was coated in lead. They peeled off a bit and saw the face of Henry III—exactly as depicted in his contemporary portraits and the tomb's effigy, fashioned from his death mask. The face was Henry's. Then—it crumbled. The body started to disintegrate on exposure to air. This excavation was made for some reason, I forget, I read it years ago but it was credible and there are pics somewhere. My point is that something that is not sensationally reported is much more believable than the daily newspapers. Also, it shows how ephemeral are human remains. Underground, unless a body is mummified, it decomposes pretty quick—definitely all gone five hundred years later, I am sure.

What about if they "found" a skeleton of King Harold with an arrow sticking out the eye?

5

Postscript to the Previous

It doesn't take me very long to detect what's going on with a news item. Got this one already. Ready? Later this year—there is planned a big mega-production of Richard III by the RSC. The news, extensively covered no doubt, will be "In the year that Richard's body was found, it is time to reassess the legacy of this great English monarch, who has been maligned for so long." Then a movie to follow? Lots of cash made by already rich people, new theater for the RSC, etc.... A great windfall.

Now this—what if the same people who cash in on the extravaganza planted the body? The report that the Richard III skeleton was dug up from beneath a car park is pretty suspicious. That seals it for me. You can't very well go digging up monasteries and protected heritage sites but you can always dig up a car park. Verdict: Richard the Turd.

What about if they dug up the bones of Prince Hamlet in Denmark... and his skeleton was holding *another* skull in its hand?

6

Hi Brett—What day is the interview? Are you going to phone me live on the radio and ask questions, or else, what do you want me to say so I can prepare. Also what time will you call?

Here's my Japan experience. I met my Japanese wife in Tokyo in early 1994 and we were married in December 1995, after a nearly two-year courtship. We lived as a regular married couple for the next fifteen years, having two daughters, Selene in 2001 and Cale in 2004. The girls are now eleven and nearly eight. In around 2009 I wanted us as a family to move away from Japan and back to England. My main reason was I wanted the girls to see more countryside and English heritage, as well as to improve their English speaking and reading skills.

The problem is, my wife did not want to leave Japan. It caused a lot of strain, and we rowed a lot.

Then suddenly in April 2010, my wife moved out and took the children to an apartment. I never saw or spoke to my children as their father again. The police would not intervene in the children's abduction—nor see their being taken away from their father as an abduction. My daughters remain to this day either kept inside their designated new apartment or marched by their mother to and from school. My daughters will not talk to me, or if I try to approach them, they run away. My wife refuses to take my phone calls or answer any e-mails. I have subsequently been warned by the police not to go near my daughters.

Having since lost my job in Japan, I moved to the United States in March 2012. From being a hands-on dad with two loving daughters who were real daddy's girls, overnight I have had no contact with my daughters for nearly three years.

I have had no sympathy, let alone assistance, from the U.S. embassy, U.S. government, or the FBI.

[This radio interview for a U.S. network was canceled. Also terminated abruptly at this time were planned interviews on the BBC and Australian news media]

7

Hello Paul [left-behind parent; LBP]—It saddens me to see your message like so many others. I don't know how to help, or what to suggest. Just the cost of going to Japan is an obstacle for many people, including myself now.

My only thought is this. It is very telling how these cruel child abusers always say: "They can see their father when they become an adult." They know that by then, it will be too late for the father to have had any influence on the child and the child will have been through Japanese school. They will be Japanese, closed off and inscrutable. They will not reach out to you.

The child abductors know this. My wife, who stole my two daughters in 2010 and, with the help of the Japanese police and family court, has prevented me all access to my two angels since that day—was extremely insecure about the girls growing up to be "western." They were both bilingual, but really their loves and interests were overwhelmingly U.S. / U.K. They loved British music, British TV shows, American movies and culture. My wife must have hated that. I think my wife was worried that as the girls grew up they would turn their backs on traditional Japan and join the outside world. Because Japan is just that—a very conventional, conservative country with an ancient culture. If you don't believe me, attend a Japanese *matsuri* (street festival) or work in a Japanese company. No one in the western world works like the Japanese. No one wears a suit constantly or stays in the office till late at night, or has nothing to do or nowhere to go at weekends. Only the Japanese live like that nowadays. A very conservative, traditional society based on male / female gender roles, respect for elders, and belief in ancient customs, such as karma and reincarnation. You can be sure that Japanese people still hold these ideas, even if they say that they don't.

OK sorry for a long aside there. If it is possible for you to travel to your child's house, now would seem the best time to go. If you can interest your child in communicating with you, there is a chance that you can gradually increase the level of that over time.

Well those are my thoughts. If I have written too much unbidden, it is because your story reminds me that I also have no avenue to my daughters.

8

It was in a small lecture theater on Berkeley campus. When [Camille] Paglia entered, to applause, I was smiling so much I must have looked like a lunatic! I noted that there were no young people in the audience—on a university campus!—

only old men with gray hair and beards and their female counterparts, mostly hippies and art lovers. I was the youngest person in the audience. Twenty years ago, the theater would have been filled with undergraduates who, like me, discovered Paglia in their youth and absorbed her brilliant message. Fame, or notoriety, doesn't last very long in America....

The presentation was in support of her new book. It took five years to write, she said at the beginning. The book is about a selection of artifacts ancient and new photographed in beautiful color frames with Paglia's thoughts on each. Paglia's message is: To those who think that God is dead, what else are you going to give to your children to believe in, in this super-saturated age of fast-moving images and senseless news items? Are you going to abandon them to confusion, or provide them with something calm and contemplative? If God is dead, then His replacement must be art. Paglia refers to herself as an atheist who has deep reverence for religion—its folk wisdom, its insight into human psychology, its basis of morality. I say to Paglia, "Then you are not an atheist." Some belief will always remain.

I took this picture after the lecture. Paglia was getting ready to sign autographs and I walked up to her and asked if I could take her pic. She said, "No flash!" Then of course my flash went off in her face, sorry! (I didn't even know my phone had a flash.) She would not look at me directly; when she spoke to me she glanced away. I wonder whether it was just me or whether she did that to everybody. I think she was shy of me somehow, because she spoke to others normally. I have read and loved her books for twenty years and have championed her as one of the most interesting thinkers and writers today—actually, the most interesting writer today. She is also an excellent speaker. I listened to her discussion enthralled. I have met a few of my heroes, person-to-person—there are only one or two I haven't encountered yet. The people whom I would like to meet, and actually I think I will, even if I have to contrive a meeting (such as by going to their public discussion, as in last night), are all approachable. For example, I love Paul McCartney but I could not get anywhere near to him, if he appeared in public. He'd be swamped by attention seekers and held back by protectors. But I think that I will meet Paul Auster one day, and Stephen Dobyns. (Probably in the same kind of situation as Paglia, a low-key book tour attended by a small number of people, for example.) But with Auster, it might be something more like a chance encounter in New York, if I went there for some reason, I'd bump into him by accident, or espy him in the street—and he would notice me and realize that I know who he is.

San Francisco, December 2012

9

I've been bedridden since Wednesday! I started feeling freezing cold, really shaking and shivering, freezing... I had to put on two sweaters and get in bed under the duvet with a hot water bottle. I was freezing—but also pouring with sweat. I kept falling asleep for just a few minutes—and had a weird dream wherein I and a group of people who were performers on a stage stood in a kind of pose—then I awoke for ten minutes before falling asleep again and having the same dream—dozens of times, all night and all through the next day, then the next night and next day.... I was delirious, I couldn't think or talk, I kept making animal noises, growling and whimpering... and I kept having to get up and drag myself up the stairs—I could hardly walk—to go to the toilet, where I did a burning hot, thick yellow piss... it was horrible. I'm better today. Not fully recovered yet. But awake.

10

I was awake again all last night. I kept having to go to toilet… so I woke up… but after finishing, I felt like there were a little bit more, so it kept me awake. I kept feeling like a little bit more wee was going to come out and pee the bed! It's really horrible. So I had to stand over the toilet waiting for little drops of urine to come out. I can't even go to see a doctor without health insurance. There are free health programs that are useless. You have to call them and leave a message, then they never call you back. Maybe the service is a way for the City to show it has care programs, which don't actually do anything. The financial resources are drained by doctors attached to the programs.

I'm fed up. I need a job and to be my own man again, with my own life and my own finances. I'm fed up. My life has just gone downhill, further and further, over the last three years. I'm praying for it to start going back uphill again, and being good.

11

I wrote about a hundred songs—all finished with chords, a melody, and lyric.

I started off talking about *Tongues in Trees*. This is my strangest album. It is the album I created as my marriage was falling apart in 2008 or maybe 2009. The line "Tongues in Trees" is from the opening speech of *As You Like It*, Shakespeare's woodland drama and the only play he set in his hometown / homeland of central England. At that time I was dying to move away from Japan. I had been living there ten years; I had two young daughters who were fascinated with English / European culture, and the only thing stopping us getting out Japan was [my wife] Keiko. That recording was made only less than half a year before Keiko was going to do something that I could not imagine were even possible then, take away Selene and Cale and turn them into who knows what. At the time I recorded *Tongues in Trees*, that was unimaginable. I couldn't imagine it were possible.

For the album cover, I put on a John Lennon white suit and beard and Selene took the photos against the trees in a nearby car park next to our house in Denenchofu.

Tongues in Trees is my saddest album.

The first song is "Solitude," another of my strange songs that only makes sense when you realize the words were written to someone who had left me in spirit years before and I was only just beginning to realize that I was living with a wife who herself stated that she only wanted my money. Also on that album is "What Road Will Take Me Home?" The song title speaks for itself! It is one of my most beautiful songs (in my opinion) and the chorus goes like this:

> You asked me to catch the Moon for you
> To hand it over on a spoon for you
> Well that's what I'm gonna try for you
> If I have to learn to fly for you

If I die and no one ever listens to my songs, I would like to be remembered for this lyric above anything else I have written in twenty years of trying to do my best for the people I opted to look after.

12

This morning, as I awoke slowly, there was a woman in my bed. Firm and real, I had my right arm loosely around her with my hand on her breast. She was asleep. I couldn't comprehend it, so my mind cast back to the previous night. Did I go out? Where am I? No, I stayed in last night. I must be in my bed at Grove Street. Who is this person lying next to me, gently breathing? I opened my eyes and confirmed that I was in bed at home, in the daylight of morning. I rolled over to look at the woman, and she disappeared. She was gone. Who was she? She was really there, a ghost. Ghosts are, I think, projections of living persons. Someone, somewhere, projected herself next to me this morning.

San Francisco, January 2013

13

Happy New Year! Guess what—I stayed in last night for a boring New Year's Eve sitting on the sofa and early retirement to bed, and now I'm back in work on New Year's Day! Last night [my brother] came round to our house and he and Mom prepared dinner and as the evening wore on they settled down to watch TV. It was clear that they had no intention of going out or even opening a bottle of wine to celebrate the New Year. And so of course I had to sit there doing that as well. They are so boring. Like old people. Except, my Mom is entitled, whereas [my brother] just chooses to live like an old person.

Last night is yet another example of something that I have been saying for quite a while now. In life, you must follow your heart. If you feel obligated to do what your family wants for you, then you are not living your own life. You are not living theirs either—you are not living anyone's life.

This year, 2013, I have got to get away from people who wish for me a life that does not suit me. Maybe you should think something along the same lines—if you feel frustrated and held back. The awful thing is, since at least 2010, and probably before that, when I still had my daughters in my life, I kept saying that I wanted to do this-and-that but never could because I was always pressured to do what other people wanted me to do. That is a mistake. I know absolutely that that is a mistake. I have lost everything, all taken away by people who helped themselves to my gifts. That is the lesson I learned since 2010: You must follow your heart.

14

Since I lost most interests in life and had nothing to look forward to in the last nearly three years, I stopped having nightly dreams or any enjoyable or interesting insights, but last night for once I had a dream to report!

It was set in India! I was in India, in a kind of Indian supermarket that you might find anywhere in London, but in the dream I was in India. There was a guru-type figure with a turban, and he instructed me to get something for a curry we were going to have. I couldn't pronounce what he said, or remember the word. I looked at all the ingredients stacked in the shop, but couldn't find the right one. I went back and asked the guru if he could write it down, but he indicated no, and instead we were all going to eat in the finest restaurant in the area. My brother Chris was there when I returned empty handed, and he complained that I failed to find the ingredient. I said I looked for it and it wasn't there, that was all. Then we went into this dark house and went up some stairs and sat in an empty room. A waiter came over and asked what I did for a living. At this point the "camera angle" of the dream panned away so that I could see myself from another view. "I" (it wasn't me but some avatar) said I was a doctor, and that I was a specialist in… dramatic pause… infectious diseases.

That was the end.

When I awoke I thought, Eh? India? Eh?

Then I got it. It was the young doctor who was me. That means work, if it is about medical anything. I got it easily. Two days ago, I e-mailed a real doctor whom I met last year to remind him I was still looking for work. He had told me to contact him in the New Year. He wrote back that he was calculating the forthcoming year's projects now, and would get back to me soon. I drove down to San Jose to meet him a few months ago—he was… Indian. The guru in my dream was him—he had the same face.
In my dream, the guru sent me on an errand, then had second thoughts and decided upon the lavish meal.

Could these visions be the deliberations of the doctor in San Jose, deciding whether to give me a job and what job? I think they were. I think the doctor has decided to give me an important job, more important than he might normally give to test a new employee, and that I will hear from him soon.

I believe that we are all psychic and that when remote persons think about others, those persons can detect their thoughts and think about them back. Our dreams contain evidence for this—if we can decode them.

15

I just got offered a job in London.

London, March 2013

16

Last week when I arrived in England, for two nights running I dreamed that I was walking and caressing my Mom-in-America's dog, Rufy. These were nondescript dream scenarios in which I happened to be walking Rufy. What strikes me, though, is I never before can remember dreaming of Rufy, and furthermore, my Mom wrote me a couple times last week to say that Rufy was missing me. If what I have been saying for years is true, that when we think of someone remotely they think of us back, then could this apply also to canines? Canines pining for their master?

17

Before I came here [returned to U.K.], because I couldn't carry it along with all the other stuff, I shipped my guitar ahead of me in the regular post. It arrived a couple weeks ago—along with a demand for £58 "VAT." I went to the post office and pointed out that since this is my old guitar which I've owned for many years, why must I pay purchase tax. He wasn't listening. He only wanted the money otherwise they were going to send it back to San Francisco. He added that I could try to claim it back using H.M. Customs' labyrinthine, incomprehensible, and unaccountable reimbursement procedure. I just paid the £58. That was on Monday. Delivery was supposed to be yesterday. It didn't arrive. Worried that they had sent it back to California despite my paying the ransom fee, I called them today. It was still in their depot undelivered. They'd send it tomorrow. No hint of an apology was detectable. Ditto this level of service with my internet provider, mobile phone, local council, landlord, electricity company, another parcel my Mom sent me, the National Insurance Office, and Barclays Bank. Since I've been abroad, do they still call this country Rip-off Britain?

18

That's right—I never said goodbye to them [my two children] because I could not suspect it were even possible for me to lose all contact with them. My wife and her accomplices planned [their abduction] in secret. If I had known, or had any suspicion, I would have taken them out of Japan. Then I would have negotiated terms of where the kids live and how they should be raised within a legal framework. I would never have pre-empted taking the kids from Keiko. Now—I would. I think she has manic mental problems and is a terrible mother as well as wife. Whether she is normal for Japan, I cannot say. I think she probably is. That is why all Japanese people support her, including the authorities. Among my last visiters at my home in Denenchofu [Tokyo] were two police officers in suits, not uniforms. They were detectives. They came round to my house and warned me not to try to go near my children. This was after the TV news filmed the girls coming out of their school and running away from me. The police arrived soon after and told me to stay away from my kidnapped children. The implication of sending detectives rather than uniformed beat officers was that there is a file on me.

19

Gene Clark had a beautiful voice and wrote many beautiful songs. He also looked like an angel somehow. He had the saddest face. But after reading his biography, it cemented what I thought of him beforehand, that his recorded music is everything that you would need to know about him. He was very quiet and introverted, unlike John Lennon or Elvis or Marc Bolan. So there are no intellectual or funny remarks or interviews. He never disclosed his song-writing ideas or influences, so there is little to learn from him about how he went about what he did. He stood for no good causes (unlike Lennon) and was not extravagantly rich nor wasteful (unlike Lennon and Elvis). We can read about Lennon's life story because it was "Grand Guignol"—a nonstop whirlwind of whims, achievements, and greatness—whereas Clark only made some beautiful records, and the rest of his life was sad and dismal and has nothing to show us and teach us.

20

This one is easy to respond to—yes inevitably they will see the world from a Japanese point of view—they were abducted and are being raised as Japanese. Cale, who has dark hair and looks more Japanese, may never feel anything but wholly Japanese for the rest of her life. Selene won't—she is almost blonde and does not look at all Japanese. I do not know for how long my girls will retain their English. I hope at least that they will find it easy to relearn even if they do not use it for a while. Remember Becky? She was some airhead TV personality in Japan, half British. Born in Japan with Japanese mother, she cannot speak any English. She behaves just like every other Japanese TV personality—guffawing at trivial rubbish and screaming instead of talking (at least while appearing on TV). I suspect that she was kidnapped by her mother and fed a load of bullshit about how her father abandoned her. I don't know this, I just suspect it. I suspect that Becky's father was pushed out, as I was, for not being a *salariman* and that Becky was overwhelmed by her mother and grandmother as a kind of cute toy and this repressive upbringing created not a level-headed, smart, beautiful woman but the stunted idiot we see on TV. I'm sitting in a coffee house in Kew in west London, surrounded by families getting ready for weekend family activities. This is an extremely well-to-do area and people are well dressed, polite, well-bred, civilized. They do not scream "*kawaiiiiii*" whenever a dog walks past nor do they chatter at great volume and keep bursting out laughing. Everyone is sitting respectably and conversing in turn. My wife's and my battle is a battle for the children's destiny and what we want for our children is mutually incompatible—what I want is to set up my children with a robust independence for their future excursions into the world. What my wife wants is for them never to leave her.

21

The idea of whether museum artifacts were bought or stolen is an interesting one. The most contested artifacts that I know are the "Elgin Marbles." These statues were procured by the British Museum from their original home on the roof of the Acropolis in Athens long ago (early twentieth century). Like the "Cleopatra Needles," the Elgin Marbles were in a state of disrepair and abandonment when the British archeologists (Lord Elgin) who found them saw their great cultural value and wished to preserve them. The problem now is that afterwards, the original owners (modern states) that wrought these artifacts have also realized their cultural value and want them back. Do you want to know what I think? The power of money rules the world and sold means sold. In addition, more people from all around the world visit the British Museum alone than ever go to Athens, and so the marbles will receive greater attention there than if they were to be returned to Greece. Finders keepers losers weepers!

22

If I were to die, and there were no Heaven, then there could be no music in death.

23

This seventeen thousand-year-old painting from Lascaux cave is in no doubt in my mind a depiction of the zodiac signs Leo, Gemini, and Taurus and suggests to me that cultural awareness of the stellar constellations as they are still known today stretches back at least that far in time. I am a strong believer [in Graham Hancock's contention] that human civilization precedes the Ice Age and I accept it is plausible that the Great Sphinx at Giza is far older than the Great Pyramids, and that the original statue was of a lion facing [the constellation] Leo's ascent in the Age of Leo (over ten thousand years ago—the pyramids are orthodoxically believed half that antiquity). Take a look at the Sphinx. The head is disproportionately small and I can accept was re-sculpted from what was originally a lion's head. I also can believe that the erosion of the Sphinx was caused by water and that since the desert does not rain this must have been melt water from the last Ice Age—again implying that the Sphinx is much older than currently contended. Finally, if the Sphinx were a statue of the pharaoh Cephre, then why does he have a lion's body? It does not make any sense. I am convinced that human civilization is older than professed by academia.

Art in the Lascaux Caves

24

In the West, rich people live off the expense of a hardworking mass majority of the population who do all the jobs but will never themselves be rich, just have enough to live on. Most workers betray little cognizance of this situation and even those who are aware, such as myself, can do nothing to change the fact so we simply acquiesce. In Japan, which I insist is female, shall we say a gyneocracy (a word I just neologized), it is not the rich but married women who live off the working population. That is why my Japanese "wife" was able to do what she did to me and the children. To her such heartless cruelty is not abnormal but natural. None of the male slaves in Japan complains, nor do the West's working slaves. Except western slaves are subject to invisible controllers to whom they are not related, whereas Japanese slaves are subject to their wives. That Japan is female is so strikingly obvious to me, that I am astonished that anyone can deny it. But propaganda blinds people.

London, May 2013

25

Hi Richard yes I would be happy to talk to you. I have some advice which you may consider. No my situation did not improve and I have been alienated from my children for three years, irrecoverable loss. My basic contention is that Japan and the West are polar opposites and that child abduction is the norm in Japan, where men are workers round the clock and children are raised by schools, not parents. Japanese culture is so formal and ceremonial that if a child gets western ideals in her head, she will be unable to concentrate on being Japanese. Japanese can only live in Japan unmixing anything into their bizarre ways.

The family court will do nothing for you. Courts are there to apply laws. There are no laws against your wife taking your children to another address, and so nothing to prove in court. Japanese people will not see why you want to raise your children, since your only concern in life as a man should be work. These are traditional, ultra-conservative people who are obsessive about preserving their culture even in the face of the rest of the world thinking how strange they are. Their smooth society works! No crime, no poverty, everyone gets a meal every night. Those are all they want. You are viewed as a disturbance. A foreigner. Japanese society will consider you a troublemaker if you wanted more from life than work. You are viewed as preventing your wife's child, who is hers not yours, from being an ardent school pupil the same as the other children, who never see their fathers either.

If you have the children's passports and can book flights for you and them and can take them, you might be able to get away with it. It depends how you appropriated them. If you took them by force, forget it. Your wife will have the police on you and you could be extradited, certainly held in custody for a while—weeks maybe. You don't want to lose your job. A better idea, if you could get away with it, is to collect the kids after school.

The Japanese family court will murder you, don't go there. The family court will side with your wife. Your wife left you because to her your influence is seen as a disturbance of your children becoming Japanese, which she believes is best for them. Stay away from the court, it will destroy you. Your case will drag on and on and come to nothing. Mine lasted eighteen months, and during that time my children were programmed against me. They used to be normal, very British, real daddy's girls. The court takes an action of dragging on cases forever while always hinting that they will be able to help you so as to prevent you from doing anything desperate, which would be a disturbance of the eternal peace, knowing that months and years of separation will wear you down until you realize the children have forgotten you.

Stay away from the court. The human rights violation of child abduction in Japan is perpetrated through the family court. One day I hope to see all these criminals (court mediators and judge) punished. Eventually Japan will abduct one child too many and the West will have to do something about it. I hear about new left-behind parents (LBPs) such as yourself every week, always confused and shattered as I was when this first happened to me.

26

If I knew before my children were abducted that that were even possible, there are many things I could have done to prevent that, including taking them out of Japan before it happened. Outside Japan, I would have brokered a fair child-rearing agreement with my wife. It would have been unthinkable for me to sever contact between my kids and their mother, something that I would not want to do even now. But I think that taking children out of Japan is a fair means to see that their contact with both parents is protected. My wife hid our children's passports months before she abducted, and must have planned it in secret, certainly with her parents' collusion. I had no notion that anyone could steal my children from me. Like most people (I guess), I thought Japan's laws were similar to British / American laws. I had heard about child abduction in Japan before, but I thought it was by people who were on the run and hiding, not people who could kidnap with the protection of the police and courts who will warn you to stay away from your taken children under threat of arrest, losing your livelihood, and extradition from Japan. Those are what I know now, and I am trying to tell everybody. Only the U.S. government can exert any pressure on Japan, and that will only happen when the scale of the problem reaches critical mass and its reasons (different culture that accepts child abduction and has no concept of the rights of children or parents as seen by western eyes) become known. I hear of a new case every week almost—the numbers must be in the hundreds or thousands and rising constantly.

27

Every cycle of the Zen philosophy can be accomplished within one lifetime—the cycles of reincarnation are just about getting older. There is nothing in Zen that cannot be learned within an average lifetime. Cycles? No way, once is enough.

28

When I turned thirty years old, Tim gave me some advisory words of wisdom as an "elder": "The difference between your twenties and thirties is, you go into your twenties young and come out young, whereas you go into your thirties young and come out old." I thought that made sense back then, but not anymore. It's your forties you enter young and come out old.

29

Last weekend, I finally did something I have been dreaming of for years—visited a crop circle! Very weird trip complete with overturned car crashed in the same field. Spent two days in Avebury, bliss.

A.R.: So, just out of interest (trying not to laugh) what is your opinion on how crop circles are created?

They've been recorded since the sixteenth century. If you laugh them off as hoaxes, go to one and see it from the ground, then calculate how you would create something intricate and symmetrical as seen from above, even on an uneven surface such as a hill plateau. My inkling is that the circles are a mystery that is not so easy to dismiss as a hoax, and that because this mystery attracts open-minded people, gets associated with cranks. A "crank" is any person who does not accept fully everything that is written in newspapers—that is, the official explanation as expounded by opinion makers who extract the most wealth from the pot.

30

Stop living your life around others and meet no expectations.

July 2013

31

To: Peter Macon, U.S. Department of State

Hello, I am a U.S. citizen whose two American daughters were abducted by their Japanese mother (who is my wife) in Tokyo in April 2010. Since their abduction, I and my family on the children's American side have been denied all contact with my daughters.

For now, all I am seeking is that my daughters' names are registered as abducted or missing at an official U.S. government level.

Child abduction in Japan is a rampant human rights violation affecting increasing numbers of Americans week by week. When will the U.S. government take steps to bring our children home? My two daughters were abducted more or less on a whim by my wife and her parents. I was given no warning; my wife and I are not divorced and nor was there any valid reason for my wife's abduction. The Japanese family court, police, the children's school, and the local community where we lived all supported my wife and stood between me and my children.

The U.S. government must step in to protect the growing numbers of American children disappearing into a black hole in Japan. The numbers of abducted American children in Japan are already in the hundreds or thousands.

Please acknowledge this e-mail with a reply.

From: The Office of Children's Issues, U.S. Department of State

Thank you for contacting us. The Office of Children's Issues is tasked with promoting the welfare and safety of children involved in international parental child abduction, and your children were not abducted or wrongfully retained across an international border. As your children have been residing in Japan, Japan is the appropriate jurisdiction for considering matters pertaining to their custody. You may wish to consider retaining an attorney in Japan who can advise you about your prospects for achieving greater access to your children under Japanese laws. These attorneys might be able to assist you to pursue greater access to your children. Please consult with your attorney before making any decision to ensure you are fully informed about your legal options and the possible ramifications of any action you consider.

Please be assured that the well-being of U.S. citizens overseas, particularly children, is one of the Department of State's highest priorities. The Office of Children's Issues, however, is not the appropriate Department of State office to provide assistance to you at this time.

To: Peter Macon, U.S. Department of State

Thank you for your prompt response.

First, my children were abducted. If someone entered your house and took your children, would you agree in that case your children were abducted? Yes, you would. You would also be very anxious that the police and law enforcement would be there to assist you, and that laws be in place to punish the perpetrators and prevent recurrence.

In Japan, there are no laws against parental child kidnapping. Child kidnappers in Japan can do as they please, and are indeed protected by the Japanese police.

I am very sure that the U.S. government is aware of this, and that the U.S. government has other reasons that on balance compel the U.S. government to turn a blind eye to this issue.

The U.S. government harming children of other nations when furthering its higher aims is regrettable enough, but the U.S. government allowing Japan to steal American children is surely the lowest, most shameful foreign policy in U.S. history. Shame on you.

August 2013

32

In last night's dream I picked up Selene and carried her around telling her that I never left her and that she was taken away from me without my consent. She listened and understood. I told her that I cried every day without her. Then we both started crying. I still am now. I will never get over the loss of my angels.

33

I had two very vivid and disturbing dreams over the weekend. On Saturday, I dreamed that I was at the top of a hill overlooking a city, and was waiting to see aircraft coming over. Actually, a few weeks ago I observed President Obama's flotilla of aircraft (Air Force One) flying into London, and on Saturday I was thinking about that, so I guess that was what inspired the dream. In the dream, I looked up, and suddenly overhead were huge alien spacecraft. These spacecraft could abruptly change shape, or open wings and solar panels. The spacecraft were really menacing and I was scared. But, everyone else seemed to be looking at them curiously and happily. I thought with such power, these aliens could kill all the human race. The spacecraft were huge, and moved instantly into different parts of the sky. I ran inside a building thinking where to hide. I thought that no one could leave the city without being seen by the aliens. I thought we were all at the aliens' mercy. Then one of the craft came down to just above the building I was in and started rattling it violently. I was terrified. That was the end of that dream. Had I had it a few years ago, I would have interpreted it as about my feeling like I were a prisoner in Tokyo, but I left Tokyo over a year ago, and I don't feel like a prisoner now. Now, I'm just numb. I don't feel anything. I have accepted all loss. I do not know what that dream represented.

The second dream was last night. It also was very vivid when I awoke this morning, but now I've forgotten the start. In the dream was my Dad. Dreams with my Dad are messages from him, because my Dad does not represent any other person but himself. They are visitations from him, as are dreams starring Selene and Cale. In this dream I had started a new job, and (with the strange background knowledge one has in dreams) had found out that what I had to do was different to what I thought I would have to do, and furthermore, my living space was a small mattress on the floor. These unwanted surprises were the fault of my Dad, who had hired me (or maybe got me a job working for him at the university). I was angry with my Dad and tried to remonstrate with him about the deception. The job and tiny living space suggest dissatisfaction with my real job and my real status of living in a one-bedroom studio flat in London. But, if so, my Dad would not be responsible in the dream. Then my Dad was drunk and falling over, as he sometimes did in later life, and I was trying to pick him up. Someone in the dream told me that he didn't want me to go, which I knew in the dream meant go to Japan to work. This dream was therefore, probably set in the 1990s when I first went to Japan and my Dad was still alive.

This second dream makes no sense to me either. Both dreams were very vivid, "message" dreams, and woke me with concern. Both dreams are similarly about my being here in London, away from family, in a job, in a house alone, they appear connected to those kinds of things. But, I don't feel dissatisfied really or in the wrong place, although I know I am displaced from my children, I feel more at home here than anywhere else except back in Denenchofu [Tokyo] with my angels. And the message from Hank, I don't know what it means.

34

I had another vivid dream last night, again work related. I was trying to get dressed for work, and looking for my clothes, and thinking they must be somewhere or other, I was searching all over. I had a faint idea that my clothes were in a suitcase, and that I had packed to go somewhere. And at the end, my American nephew Olin appeared. I told him not to play outside an old school. That was the end of the dream. Today is six months since I arrived in England. My return flight back to U.S. departs this morning, and I'm not on it.

35

I just came out with one of my typical jokes that earned me nothing but hatred! I was in the wine shop and said to the matronly assistant I wonder whether you stock a certain California wine I like. We went over to the Cali wines and she said to me, how oak-y is it? I playfully quipped, "No, California!" She looked at me with ice-cold daggers! I almost never get any reward for my jokes. I usually receive a polite, oh ha ha, but never a laugh worthy of how good they are!

36

Early during my career at Elsevier [in Japan], there was only one other foreigner who ever worked there, for a short while, a Frenchman who joined the finance department or some type of management. The thing I remember about him the most, was he had an obsequious manner of speaking in Japanese always and really putting on the Japanese behavior, bowing properly and pretending to be Japanese. He was quite unctuous. He also had a Japanese wife and child, and I remember he always told me that his family drove around the isles of Japan a lot at weekends, mostly visiting their various friends in different parts of the land. This man had truly been incorporated into Japan. He left the company ages ago and I never saw him again, until recently, when he re-surfaced in Japan's fastest-growing ex-pats club—the Left-Behind Parents (LBPs) of Japan. This Frenchman signs his writing on LPB-dom "Loving father whose children were abducted in 2003." So ten years ago, when he was doing his best to become accepted by Japan, his wife still stole their child. Child rearing in Japan is the sole responsibility of schools; mothers help the schools but really only schools have any say in a child's upbringing. Fathers are removed from children by their workplaces. They have to stay in their workplaces till late at night because they are not allowed to be at home.

37

There was a lot of furore and debate last week concerning Real Madrid buying Gareth Bale for €100m while "twenty-five percent of Spain's young people are unemployed" and Spain's economy is "in ruins." As for me, I think a €100m footballer is great. If Real Madrid took that money and donated it to Spanish unemployed people, let's say five million people, they would each receive €20— enough for a pizza night out and then all that money is gone. The reason we have beautiful artworks and gorgeous churches and palaces is that wonderful things cost money. Either rich people commission beautiful paintings or communities get together and each donate a small amount to build a magnificent edifice. And having the world's most expensive footballer is better overall for the Spanish unemployed than a small cash injection. On the other hand, giving a huge amount of money to a vulgar lottery winner to go mad on overspending on tasteless junk and lavish accumulation of cars and holidays is the opposite of patronizing the arts: that is the community clubbing together to fund a monster.

38

What did you, like, say?

The "like" trope / verbal hesitation has infectiously taken hold here in U.K. In San Francisco it's ubiquitous. None of the people who say it every other five words appears aware that it carries a stigma of "inarticulate." It has simply replaced "And then I said…." Language evolves!

39

In last night's dream, I was on a train. I was with a mate on the train (don't know who it was), who said he was going to jump off at the next stop, which was in some woods, and pick up his kid. The train stopped, he got off, then the train started again and left him on the platform with his kid. I heard in my head (in this dream) that he said he would get the next train. Then I was at the front of the train, speeding through countryside, reclining back, sitting next to two girls. The girl next to me brushed her hand against mine. Although I was excited, I kept looking dead ahead on this train journey. I thought, does this train go home? Yes, I remembered that it did.

I woke up. The girl in the dream was a girl at football [soccer] yesterday. I played an all-day football competition at MRC [former workplace] on Mill Hill—my first return in two decades. An old friend who still works there invited me. At the football was a pure delight, a blonde Austrian girl. We noticed each other (I couldn't keep my eyes off her) and I chatted to her a couple times. She knew I liked her. She showed me her bottom! (Bent over and gave me a look.) My word she was hot. And what did I do? Held back as always, and finally at the end of the event went home. The train dream was my missing her. Maybe my mate who missed the train was my missing the train as usual. It was certainly that girl in the dream.

One last thing. Remember Vienna kept coming up last weekend, and I was convinced that something connected to Vienna would culminate this weekend. Vienna, Austria? I didn't even ask the girl where in Austria she was from.

I've got to pull myself together and stop missing things. I'm becoming the biggest loser on the planet.

40

Season of loneliness for me—September thru November. I'm hoping to go Japan beginning of October (Selene's birthday, and the girls' school sports day is my only real guarantee of seeing them). I am also going to talk to them.

I have to win. There is no other way. My life rests on this kamikaze mission. I win my girls, or I die. I don't mean I expire, but I die inside. I have been un-dead since I lost them. I cannot keep returning to Japan in order to try to smile at my girls if they have been trained not to talk to me and a *salariman* is not important in their lives. This is my last mission. *Banzai!* Kamikaze.

41

In my nightly dreams about Selene and Cale, they get bigger and more mature in appearance and can still speak English. In last night's dream Cale was a beautiful young woman with very gold hair. She looked like nothing I have seen in real life: the Cale she must be now. I will soon find out, when I see them for the first time in over one year, whether the girls in my dreams are visitations / communications from them or illusions. I never dream about the small children I actually remember, and our nightly dream encounters are all about our current state of separation, not going back in time to when I knew their every day.

42

Everyone has secrets. You can share some secrets with only one person, and keep those secrets from others. You are the curator of your secrets! That is why you are so mysterious, because you have secrets. All clever people have secrets. I never tell my secrets to anyone I don't like—they don't deserve to hear them. My books impart a lot of my secrets, and only a few people choose to read my books. The rest are not worthy of my secrets! I know many friends in Japan who got married [to Japanese wife or husband] and are starting to raise their children in Japan, and they are all heading for deep trouble without knowing it. My book [*Life & Nihonjin*] is there to warn them, but they are not interested. On the other hand, one person contacted me because he was worried about his wife's behavior and losing his baby boy. I gave him my book, he read it, and thereupon decided to leave Japan with his baby.

43

In dreams, my nightly meetings with my daughters and occasional meetings with my Dad (who passed away 1996) feel very real encounters. For a start, unlike many of the characters in my dreams, my daughters and Dad are not representatives possibly of other people or feelings. They represent themselves and are, I believe, themselves. I suspect that they are caused by my daughters thinking about me or dreaming about me simultaneously with my sleep. As for my Dad, it seems as though his spirit exists.

Tokyo, October 2013

44

Here are today's activities [in Japan]. This morning I went to the school early 7:30 but evidently missed them because by eight o'clock I didn't see them. They must have gone in extra early, lots of kids were pouring in even at 7:30. I returned at 3 p.m. to see them coming out and once again saw hundreds of kids pour out but not Selene and Cale. I asked the security guard why they hadn't emerged and he said because of me they didn't want to come outside. So I waited. I expected Keiko to come and get them but she didn't. I walked the couple hundred yards down the road to their apartment which sounded empty so the girls were definitely still inside the school. I returned to the school and waited another hour till 5:30 then once again went down to the apartment and this time they were there, I could hear them inside. They can only have gone out the school by some back exit. This is not the first time the girls have been spirited out the school when I was waiting at the gate. There is a back exit used for these types of ruses, certainly a lot of excluded parents throughout Japanese society and hidden escape routes at Japanese schools to secrete children in and out. I'll be back on the street tomorrow morning at 7:00.

45

B.G.: Alex, how did it go today, trying to see your daughters?

Didn't see them, being held in police station now. Welcome to Japan. It's been such a pleasure.

46

B.Z.: Since words are not appropriate now [while you are being held in custody], as an academic teacher of Japanese Studies, I don't know how to face my students and what to tell them about Japan….

Just teach your students how to speak Japanese. If they ask what is family in Japan, tell them family does not exist. If they ask you whether it is a good idea to marry a Japanese person, say no, and if they want to live in Japan, say Japan is Hell, so go there, take what you need, and get out, like Orpheus, and don't look back.

47

This morning once again I waited for Selene and Cale and this time they emerged with their kidnapper [mother]. As they walked past me, Selene said on cue, "Don't come to my school." No please, no Daddy. She sounded like a Japanese person trying to speak English. Then all of a sudden a *salariman* [Japanese worker] wearing a janitor uniform was trying to stand between us. I told him to fuck off but he still hovered around. The girls went into the school and I walked back with Keiko, just talking to her with this horrid little caricature walking along with us as well. We all walked down the street and finally Keiko went into her apartment. As I walked away, still followed by the *salariman*, who was pestering me, I found myself surrounded by more and more police officers who, in the customary Japanese way, started to ask me whether I would voluntarily go to the police station. The way this works is they keep asking you and meanwhile a police car arrives ready to put you in. I said I would go to the police station if I can talk to my wife.

So I ended up in the police station being grilled as to what was I doing. I must have said trying to see my daughters and give them their birthday presents about a hundred times. Then they insisted that I agree not to go to the school or try to see my daughters again. They decide this for you. And they keep you in the police station indefinitely till you agree. I was on the phone to the British embassy throughout, saying I want to leave the police station. The embassy reassured me that the police said I was not arrested and could leave any time. But when I went to walk out, they ran in front and blocked the exit. Keiko arrived and I spoke to her for the first time in four years. She just repeated the same demands as in the family court, that she wants a divorce and this and that, and that the children don't want to know me. So I've got my daughters saying they don't want me to go to their school, the police threatening me to stay away, and my wife demanding things and telling me my daughters are scared of me. My daughters are the possessions of these barbarians. Only one thing truly mattered to me today. The rest I've heard before many times. But today I learned that my baby Cale has been going to a mental clinic. That was too much. When they told me that, my coffee cup fell out my hand. What have these Stone Age trolls done to her? I can't take this country where everyone suffers any more.

Keiko told someone who told me. Cale was so sensitive and always needed her Daddy. She wet her bed right through to about six years old. She is hilarious and needs good-humored people to adore her. She is surrounded by cruel robots and probably told to shut up instead of be funny. She cannot understand why she was taken away from her home and kept in a prison prevented from mentioning her Daddy. She has been kidnapped, it's no wonder she is suffering.

48

To: Carl Frater, British Consul Tokyo

Hello, this is a message for vice consul Carl Frater. I have asked the British embassy to complain about my treatment by Tokyo Metropolitan Police on October 2nd. I would like to add that apart from my detainment at Denenchofu police station for a few hours I was also coerced to state that I would not in future go near my children's school, despite the road on which I was apprehended being a public thoroughfare. So my question is, what law did I break by waiting to see my children, and why were about twenty armed riot police sent to intervene? As far as I am aware, looking at one's own children in a public space is not illegal. It would be nice if the British embassy inquired to the police why I was told not to try to see my kids. I was in no way disturbing the peace. Lastly, please ask the police permission for me to attend my children's sports day on Saturday—one of the main reasons I traveled to Japan at considerable expense this week.

From: British Consul

Thank you for your e-mail. Carl is out of the office until Wednesday, so I will reply to your e-mail. We called Denenchofu Police Station and tried to speak to the officer in charge of your case to ask about the statement and if you would be able to go to the school sports day. Unfortunately, due to several serious incidents in the area, there were no officers available to discuss the specifics of your case. We did ask them, in general terms, if there would be any repercussions if you went to the school, and the officer said it would be likely that the police would be called to the school.

For your questions about the law, specifically, waiting to see your children in a public place, definition of disturbing the police, I would suggest that those questions are best put to a lawyer.

Finally, thank you for giving your permission for us to use your experience to speak with the National Police Agency to clarify their procedures for voluntary questioning. We will be contacting them in due course. If you wish to make a complaint to the police about your experience, you can write directly to Tokyo Metropolitan Police.

Dear Consular Assistant—Thank you for getting back to me, but your reply is depressingly unsatisfactory.

When the British embassy asks questions on a British national's behalf, I expect answers. Why was no one specifically involved in the case available to answer, and what were these "serious incidents" that kept them too busy to respond? Someone dropped some litter? Have you ever been to Denenchofu?

Did any of the officers involved in the case return your call subsequently, or did the embassy try again?

I want to know why I was arrested and held by the police, warned not to try to approach my children, and told not to attend my daughters' sports day, not be fobbed off with "find yourself a lawyer."

The police are acting beyond the law and complicit in the human rights violation of child abduction in Japan.

I would be grateful if you pursued this matter until an answer is provided and if not, note that your inquiries were blocked by very dubious excuses, for the official record.

[No further reply from British embassy Tokyo]

49

After I was held by the police for a few hours and released, they phoned me to say that my wife would talk to me again at the police station on the Friday, so I went back there that day. We met in the police station with a guard sitting nearby, but no one was listening to us. Keiko had (as usual) a piece of paper which serves as a divorce paper in Japan. Basically, if both spouses sign it, you're divorced. Keiko wanted me to sign it. I said you must be joking. I have no idea what that entails for me. How can a divorce paper not include any reference to the children and assets (our house which I am ten years into repaying the mortgage). I asked my wife why she wanted me to sign it so badly. She said that she wanted to move on. I said do you wish to remarry? She replied yes. I asked to whom? She said no one yet, but wanted to remarry. She indicated that a match agency can find her a partner. Sounded not true to me. I suggested that she already has a partner and wants to marry him? She denied it. I also asked her whether she has had someone for years, even before we split up? That would most neatly explain everything that happened to our marriage. She denied that, for once quite convincingly so I have to believe her. But I do not believe that she has no one lined up now. In Japan, it is highly probable that a marriage is for convenience. So I can understand one of Keiko's main aims is to remarry. But I do not know how my getting a divorce will affect my permanent resident's visa, for example, or ownership of my house. I simply don't have access to information that allows me to make an informed decision. I would allow Keiko a divorce if it softened her towards my regaining contact with my girls, but only if it did not make her then able to claim ownership of the house, for example. I know what Japan is like. I already discovered that in the eyes of Japanese law, I was *never* married to my wife, despite that we were married in U.K. and our marriage is therefore legally recognized in U.K.; in Japanese law, I am only registered as a guest of my wife's family in Japan. Marriage between Japanese and non-Japanese is a "special arrangement" and not really marriage. Anyway, I promised Keiko that I would look into it.

During our two-hour talk, here are some of the following bits I remember: I asked, "Don't you think you have hurt the children by not allowing them to see their father?" "No! They were so happy when we moved out! They kept thanking me!" When Keiko says things like that, she is the opposite of convincing. Her body language reveals she feels a lot of distress lying. She smiles and raises her hands in the air like an evangelical fanatic. I prefer to go by her body language. When I said to her that brainwashing children against their father is wrong, she replied that all parents more or less brainwash children, as part of raising them. I said there is a difference between raising children according to accepted norms and lying to them. Teaching children is not the same as brainwashing them. When I asked Keiko why is it that Selene and Cale cannot speak to their grandmother in the States, Keiko at first did not reply, but ten minutes later came up with this: "When I invited Meme to our apartment not long after I took the children there, I went to great lengths to prepare a nice meal for her. But when she came to our apartment, she brought a bag containing only two ice creams for the children. After she left, the girls said they could not believe that Meme brought ice cream only for them and not for me (Keiko). They never wanted to speak to her again." When I suggested that Meme [Keiko's name for her mother-in-law, my Mom] brought ice cream for the children because ice cream is usually thought of as children's food, which many adults don't eat because it is fattening, Keiko still could not see the absurdity of children stating that they do not want to see their grandmother ever again for failing to bring their mother an ice cream. Keiko's ideas about what the children think and say are "voices in her head" category. She has a personality disorder, I think, and a selfishness that cannot consider anyone but her own narcissism. Keiko also told me that Selene went to her and said she wants to change her name from Kahney to Ono (Keiko's family name). This sounds to me, along with most things Keiko says, that at first she thinks something then either tells her captives what she thinks until they repeat it back or maybe doesn't even do that and then her idea becomes in her mind the girls' idea originally. I mean, have you ever heard a child spontaneously say that she wants to change her name? Maybe Keiko suggested that having a foreign name might not be good for her in future, so that Selene (in response to the loaded statement) then retorted that she should change her name. In any case, I know that my daughters are thoroughly brainwashed because everything I am reported by Keiko that they say about me was unthinkable before they were kidnapped.

In Japan, Keiko can do what she wants with police protection. In the 1930s, white people could serve the same injustices on black people in places like Louisiana. That's what Japan is today. My sortie to Japan last week I described before I went as a "kamikaze mission." That meant, I regain contact with my daughters or stop tormenting over it. I will always love my angels and want them back, but I am not going to waste time in a losing battle to get them on my own. I will continue to ask the British and American governments to help, but that's all from my end, for the time being anyway. I'm just going to wait for my daughters to find me.

London, November 2013

50

I was walking in the grounds of Syon House today when a top-notch Eastern European-looking chick appeared with a nerdy bloke who was carrying photography equipment. She was wearing a short skirt and was very leggy. I spotted her a mile off. Five minutes later, I was walking through another part of the garden when these same two stepped out in front of me and walked in my direction ahead of me. They stopped at a secluded corner and as I passed them she span round and caught my eye. She was *hot*. There seemed no changes of clothes for her to put on so this was not a fashion shoot. That only leaves one thing, I guess. I carried on walking and reached a shut gate so turned round and headed back. An old perv (not me, another old perv) had ensconced himself on a convenient bench near to the pair. The camera nerd was setting up a tripod and she was standing around. As I walked past, she got down on her haunches right in front of me—my sunglasses steamed up! This was all set beside a narrow lake, and to keep going I had to cross a bridge and walk along the other bank. It was here that I took the picture of the statue I sent you earlier. Across the lake, I could espy the photographer feverishly snapping the girl, who was obscured from view by a willow tree. I wonder what she was revealing to the camera. In that brief fifteen minutes, in the grounds of a stately home with a statue on a pedestal and an unobtainable young princess, I walked into my story [unpublished novel] I wrote nearly twenty years ago.

51

Japan has never had a revolution. The Meiji Revolution was not a revolution, but a reformation. Revolutions stem from the masses and are aimed against oppressive rulers. The Meiji reformation was directed from the rulers down at the people. Therefore the Meiji reformation was a totalitarian movement, although it improved the living conditions of Japanese people. Japanese common people have never in all history tried to help themselves.

A revolution is a total mass advance toward a better life by everyone, including taking arms and fighting, or dying, for that right. Every revolution cost its victories in blood. There will never be a revolution of people who either say "Yes boss" or sleep.

December 2013

52

It took a couple hours to get there [Sudbury, Suffolk] on train so by the time I arrived it was just getting dark. Magical country. Saw loads of Gainsborough masterpieces at the Gainsborough house, and found the tree depicted in *Mr. and Mrs. Andrews* [painting] which is still growing in the garden of the family home two hundred fifty years later. After, I cycled a short way to the nearby hamlet of Borley—location of Britain's Most Haunted House, Borley Rectory (burned down 1939) and famously haunted church. Arrived on my bicycle just as the last light faded. Place was deserted. And very scary. There was a real atmosphere of gloom. I don't know what I was thinking, going there on a bicycle. There have been reports of ghost nuns, carriages, noises, strange lights, automatic writing on walls, and heavy objects thrown at people from nowhere. I was on my bike! I attempted to walk round the church but I couldn't do it. The atmosphere was too forbidding. The church is twelfth century but its dedication (saint) has been forgotten over the centuries. It's just "Borley Church."

53

One time I bet James I could run all the way up BSI [former workplace] stairs twice (I don't know why it was twice and not once or thrice). Anyway, I did it. I remember James's face looking up the stairwell getting smaller and smaller as I ascended. I ran up the seventeen floors the first ascent two steps at a time, but when I ran back down and had to do it again I ran up the second time one stair at a time. What a feat of youth! And just for… a laugh during work.

London, May 2014

54

Dear Zac Goldsmith [Member of Parliament for Richmond Park, London]

The recent visit of Japanese prime minister Shinzo Abe to Britain and the resultant joint statement from the two countries' prime ministers prompted me to write to you today.

I lived in Japan for a dozen years (since have returned to my native U.K.). In 2010, my Japanese wife abducted our two children, then aged eight and six, and I never saw them again. They went from two normal, very British, fluent in English children to I don't know what they are now.

Child abduction is rife in Japan. Japanese parents, predominately mothers, are allowed to take children from the other parent and that parent is then supposed to get lost. The Japanese police have arrested me for trying to see my children, and the school wherein they are kept all day every day will call the police if I am spotted.

One day, I was suddenly out my children's lives. Japanese society—where men work till late at night every day and have little to do with their children—is designed for child abduction.

Please look into this issue. The British embassy in Tokyo is well aware of the numbers of British children who are withheld away from their British parent in Japan.

This is a cultural chasm of family values.

What our abducted children need is a champion of their human rights within the U.K. government.

Please do something about this. Will the U.K. government allow its children to be robbed without saying a word?

From: Zac Goldsmith, MP

Thanks for getting in touch and for sharing your story with me. I'm appalled to hear of your experiences. With your permission, I will contact the Home Office to ask their advice. In the meantime, the Government have provided information on Child Abduction in Japan following the introduction of the "Hague Convention," which came into force last month. I should point out that within the document, it is stated that "the British government cannot, under any circumstances, force the taking parent or the Japanese courts to return a child to the country where they normally live."

Dear Zac Goldsmith—Thank you for responding so positively and quickly. At the time of the abduction (April 2010) and for the next two years until I eventually had to leave Japan, I worked tirelessly through Japanese family court visits, advocating the Japanese government, the British embassy Tokyo (especially Vice Consul Carl Frater), the press including the BBC, and many other news organizations around the world.

I am aware that the British government cannot interfere with other countries' legislation, and that recently Japan signed the so-called Hague Convention. The Hague will not be applied retroactively and it does not apply to my children's case.

I have tried everything. What is needed here is something new. That's why I am appealing to you, my MP. It needs someone in a position of power to raise this issue with the government of the U.K.

I and many others have lost our children. My wife over a period of a few years went insane, for want of a better word. In the end, living with her was unbearable—that is, when I was allowed inside the house. She moved out suddenly and stole all our savings (possibly over £100,000). When I first went to the police, the desk officer laughed. I received not a word of sympathy from any Japanese person, and there is no legal or even social apparatus available within Japan for "left-behind parents" to obtain any access to their children. My children are marched to school each morning, spend all day there, then are marched home to a tiny apartment and locked in there all night till the next day. They are prisoners. And they had no say in what happened to them because my wife suddenly did this (with the help of her parents).

OK that's enough for now. I don't want to overwhelm you. Please, please look into this. The internet is replete with reports of child abduction in Japan. This issue could be solved by embarrassing Japan to sort out this problem. The United States is the nation by far the most affected by child abduction with at the very least three hundred left-behind fathers (mostly, and some mothers) who have been unable to see or speak to their children for years. We have no voice. If the British and American governments even conversed about this, it would soon come to an end.

55

Just listening to "Flowers in the Window." Remember that song? It's a nice song, a bit Beatles-y. That band came and went (can't even remember their name). Due to that one hit, we can be sure they never had to work in an office. I wrote a hundred songs that were all better (catchier, more original and engaging) than "Flowers," with its rather trite imagery (flowers withering like love!). There are no professional recordings of my songs, so they remain unheard as they could be. Even the six songs I cut on 208 Records were recorded in a rush, unrehearsed. When The Beatles recorded their first album "in only twelve hours," they performed songs from a six-year constant live repertoire.

Yes I'm fed up. Just had an argument with my "boss" (as if anyone bosses me) and now I'm sitting in a café after walking out. I've got rent to pay—the only reason I get up to go to work. Fed up. I wonder if there are any undiscovered islands I could live on. Preferably with an all-female tribe in fur bikinis....

56

Only young people can make music. It is not that composers use up their melodies. The celebration of music is sexual and primaveral.

57

I'm sitting outside nice pub now. There's some Lancashire type effing and blinding to his cronies on next table. Neolithic primate.

I read an interesting piece on the origin of language among humans essayed by the great Ted Hughes, in which he argued words such as aggression and aggravation etc. derive from the feral "*Grrrr.*" I reckon among the Angles and Saxons there was already the word fuckin'.

There's a mixed bunch of students (high school I think, not even uni), all drunk, in here now doing ten-strong clustered "selfies" all with pouting "duck-faces." How great it is to be young. Why? The competition among young people is for popularity. The competition among grown-ups is survival.

When you're young, you don't have baggage. I'm looking at youngsters laughing at this and that, here in this Wetherspoons pub in Salisbury, above which is a BnB wherein I stayed with my wife and kids before I lost them five years ago.

By the way, you should read my book [*Life & Nihonjin*]. Only the first third is a selection of our daily exchanges (all still good). The rest is my illumination from living in an opposite culture, by which I became transformed—perfectly fine to be a loser, although riddled with regret. East and West, high and low, male and female—opposites that we must assimilate and align.

58

With all this time on my hands [I was sacked from my job at Niche for "misconduct"] I re-read Wilde, perused a good book about his life, and paid my respects outside his 1890s home on Tite Street. As I have done, he was a little too witty and well dressed for the average man and they got together to bring him down. I lost everything. Wilde was in a more elevated position than I will ever be, and so he fell a lot further. I am currently of no use to anyone. I didn't ask to lose my family, home, or job, and nor did I deserve those trials. I began, not finished, by blaming myself. But now I do not know the reasons.

59

Every law in the U.K. has been passed with the same aim, to protect the wealth of those who have it. This originally meant the ruling classes, but nowadays encompasses anyone who makes it rich—businessmen, property owners, and the like. Have you ever wondered why the Highway Code is a code and not law? It is so that the police, those faithful servants of the ruling rich, can flout it without "breaking the law." I just observed a police car doing about 100mph jump through a series of red lights, in pursuit of some chav to put him in his place no doubt. I got fined £50 for cycling on the sidewalk, not obstructing anyone, the other day. Meanwhile, wealthy BMW and Mercedes drivers can ignore speed limits and jump red lights with impunity. If you ever need the assistance of the police for any reason, put on a navy blazer and affect an haughty accent before you enter the police station. Otherwise they won't help you.

60

The founder of [small-time medical communications agency] Niche, Tim, soon after I started work there told me he knew the "cure for diabetes." I said well-done Tim, good work I'm sure that millions of diabetologists and patients doing their best to manage the horrible symptoms of that condition will be pleased to hear it. "Bariatric surgery," he continued. I pointed out that bariatric surgery is indicated in a very small number of very obese patients who have failed attempts to lose body weight by diet and exercise and are in greater danger of obesity-related morbidity and mortality than of the highly invasive, very expensive, and hazardous surgery itself. Tim was not listening. I added that although overweight and obesity are known causes of diabetes, not all diabetic patients are overweight and gastric banding in these individuals seems inappropriate. He still was not listening. That's because he is a dick. Every single project he possessively and obsessively brought into that company was branded with crackpot notions. Once he managed to get a client who wanted us to write a human nutrition course—then after I delivered it, the client wanted to add subsections on how coconut water was a proven cure for AIDS. I found out that the client was a born-again Christian with a following of cultists in Florida—the kind of crank that somehow knew where to find Tim and whom Tim was unable to assess as a crank.

Tim has fuddled through acceptance by associating with similar people—the village idiots on the outskirts of science. Every project I did for Tim at Niche had this same crank-signature. Need further examples? Justin, my manager, asked me to "edit and rewrite as much as you can" a piece he himself had previously written. It was a review of some treatment for a client's website, but Tim had taken a liking to it and had suggested that Justin try to publish it in a journal. I did some research and quickly discovered that Justin had plagiarised it word for word from another published article. Knowing that if accepted by a journal, the plagiarised author would soon find out, Justin needed me to disguise it. Need more examples? There are plenty more. Simply, the company is a bunch of amateurs, and Tim is thick. He (early on) gave me a piece of writing he had been working on intermittently for some years and asked if I could develop it. It was garbage, badly written crap. I rewrote the entire thing, I had to. It went from unpublishable, incomprehensible, meaninglessness tripe to a good article. Of course Tim never forgave me. It happened time and time again, where I had to fix messes at the company. Tim avoided me, he couldn't stand me. Worse still, he knew my attitude to the company, my salary, and the lack of a bonus last December was spreading discontent among the other lowly paid, female, junior writers he could only hire and the dissent had to be silenced by sacrificing its source. In the end, I gave Tim the excuse he needed. So I got fired. Tim's solicitor assured him that he could make up a crime I committed and not have any reprisal—the Tories changed the law for eligibility for unfair dismissals appeals to be granted only to employees with two years' service rather than the previous one year's service, giving more power to business owners and less to workers, as is the Tories' style.

So I got the boot by that moron. I'll get him back. What goes around comes around. He owes me a bonus and a shortfall of how much I should have been earning for the last year and a half, and also he needs to find out what it's like to lose his job and face dole [unemployment benefits]. I will get these revenges by taking away his clients as much as I can. I reread "The Cask of Amontillado" the other day and I understand perfectly why the lifetime-unpublished Poe ended his writing career with a tale of revenge.

61

I'm in the dole office now—wringing my cap for housing benefit. Last week I applied for a job as senior medical writer at Springer and after completing my "writing test" (they never try to read my published work just make applicants perform a demeaning test), they wrote back in the usual corporate terms which they believe are business-like but reveal how treacherous they are: "We feel that his writing is not of the requisite standard for senior medical writer and feel (they always say feel) that his application would be more suited to medical associate (where recent grads start)." I knew the real reason and this was confirmed when I went for the interview—the incumbent senior medical writer had not one jot of my ability and experience. I talked her out the room, she didn't have a chance against me. I talk, think, and write as a medical expert, unlike everyone else in med comms. This morning I was sent their list of excuses not to hire me, all bullshit.

Eight years ago, when I was involved in Astra Zeneca's educational program for the antiandrogen drug Casodex, the trials' principle investigator—Professor Akaza, Japan's (and one of the world's) foremost prostate cancer specialist—would phone Elsevier and insist that I and no one else wrote each manuscript. That was where I was eight years ago. For some reason I am now the million-pound check that no one will cash. I don't know for how much longer, but I'm hoping that, after four bad years, it will end this week. That writing test that you didn't read, if commissioned at a med comms agency by a pharmaceutical company, took me three hours to write and would command upwards of $5,000. A full manuscript, which would take me five working days, upwards of $10,000. I want those rewards for myself.

September 2014

62

I had a weird day where I had to wait extra-long for everything. Crossing the railway at the level crossing at Richmond took ages both there and back. Went to the cycle shop and waited interminably while customers hogged the few staff. At the gym I had to wait for each machine for ages, then when I got home I realized I'd left my phone in the gym and went back—only to find everyone outside for fire alarm and waited ten minutes to go in. These delays are connected to my starting at GSK next week and my constant stressing about it. They seem to be telling me to be patient and stop worrying. Another thing happened today, cycling in slow-moving traffic I got distracted by a busty blonde pedestrian and crashed into the back of the car in front, which had stopped at a zebra crossing. After that, for the first time in days I was able to think about something else except GSK. All things happen for a reason, or seem to happen for a reason—which is the same thing.

63

One time (in a fit of envy) [an old work colleague] Danvers went behind my back to my manager with some little complaint about me, I forget what, resulting in my manager giving me "a word." I forget all that was said, except he intimated that "Danvers and you (me) are very similar in many ways." That was the second time in my life that I was compared to someone whom I disregarded as my opposite. That's quite a good lesson actually, that how you perceive people and how you yourself come across are observed by others in unknown ways. It's probably true that if any third party says you are similar to someone, then any other person who knows you both would likewise agree. Anything that anyone tells you about you is worth considering, especially anything you don't like.

64

Excellent Freudian paraphraxis by the lady giving a presentation I'm enduring at GSK right now. Talking about a merger with Novartis, she just said, "And so those are the key values that we are going to drop, er, I mean adopt."

65

Four people sitting next to me in Maids café, men and women, my age or above, teachers apparently from overheard snippets, having a gossip. One of the teachers must teach teenagers because she keeps inflecting her contributions with teen talk. Embarrassing. Every particle of their conversation during the last half hour is inspired by what's in the news. If you take apart a Sunday broadsheet, you will find the latest news, what's-on, property, business, sports. Enough to feed all your thoughts for the week....

If you are a sheep. I'd rather read a book written a century ago, full of wisdom.

That Freudian slip I heard the other day, I am very sure that no one else picked it out, including the person who uttered it. To them it was just a slip of the tongue, immediately forgotten. To me, it was an indication of what the bosses at the company secretly intend to do. So who is better informed? Among the two most important books I read when young were Freud (interpretation of dreams, id & ego, paraphraxes) and Rochefoucauld. Those books provided me insights that put me on another level from people who are unaware of what those books can tell us. And I owe those lessons to Freud and Rochefoucauld: not my superior cleverness, theirs.

66

Do you think you look better in the mirror than in pictures? I think I look great in the mirror but in photos I look like one of the Mr. Men! It's probably because you position yourself in best angle in the mirror, which a pic (or everyone around you) doesn't do. I must look alright though, several young women walked into me / brushed me (a telltale sign) and a few spontaneously talked to me today. Here's one. I stopped in the street to read my *London Walks* book on a route I was following, when a young lady in jogging gear stopped next to me. It was a bit weird. She took off her earbuds and asked me where I wanted to go. I told her, and as she pointed the direction I saw that she was clutching an incongruous pair of high heels in her hand. I thanked her and added, why you holding those (with a smile), to which she replied, frostily, "Because I am"—just as her boyfriend appeared! Women!

67

[On *Magic in the Moonlight*] I watched it last week. I guess Woody is trying to say there is no magic—except love. The newspaper reviews here [U.K.] were all complaining that Colin Firth is old and Emma Stone is young, something that the nation is very anti.

68

You shouldn't listen to the news, I don't! There's a sad case here of a schoolgirl who has gone missing. I only know because I noticed posters on lampposts and shop windows everywhere from her parents asking her to come home. She went missing in Brentford. Now the papers have zoomed in on the main suspect, an Eastern European who murdered his wife in 1998 and has gone AWOL recently. I'm not so sure he killed this schoolgirl (if she is dead but it looks pessimistic). Men who murder their wives (and *vice versa*) were driven nuts to do so. They don't have the same evil, malignant psychopathology of child killers, or rapists. My point is the news turns everything into what it is not.

69

Thank you for saying those [critical comments on *Life & Nihonjin*]. It's such a weird book. Written in bizarre circumstances, I kind of channeled it. It's really hard pointing a finger at [Japanese] people and saying they're this and that. I had to go through the entire manuscript adding "or so it seems to me" after every accusation / observation. Funny how so many people say, "I like the unusual format but no one else would!" I gave up trying to think the book would sell years ago. I have a feeling that it will be discovered one day. So many of my favorite books and writers enjoyed no success in their own time. No, I'm not comparing myself to Poe, only acknowledging that some books need to sit on the shelf for a while before someone takes a look. That part of my life tore out my heart and I still bear the scars, although they are getting better. I need to move on, and my new business is just the tonic. One day my phone will ring and I'll hear the name Daddy again.

70

What actually happened was following my *unfair* dismissal at Niche, I told the dole office I'd been made redundant. Depending on their investigation, they'd either give me my rent or tell me to F-off. I took a gamble, and while I was job hunting, didn't pay my rent for a month, then two months, then three months.... Finally the dole agreed to pay my rent. So I spent the money they gave me on my normal accustomed lifestyle (champs / fine takeaways). Nothing went right on the job front, and it looked like I would have to go back to the U.S. penniless. Then at the very final minute (11:59:59 p.m.), I got the offer from GSK. I was in a state of utter desperation. At one point, I told my landlord that I might be moving out in September, but probably not (I didn't mention that I'd been fired, and was just praying that I'd get a new job soon). A few days before I got the call at GSK, my landlord called me that since I might be moving out, they had found a new tenant and that I would be thrown out unless I resumed paying my rent forthwith. I had been evicted. I had lost everything, every single thing! My job, my home, my family. I was completely penniless—actually in a lot of debt (on my credit cards). I was also in a continual fearful state that my benefits would be stopped (you cannot claim if you were fired for "misconduct"), or that GSK would ask Niche for a reference and find out why I left, and chop my contract. I was perpetually insecure, night and day. I hit rock bottom. Then I got saved.

October 2014

71

This e-mail is about a girl named Beth. When I started at GSK, Beth gave me loads of attention. Every time I looked up she had her eyes on me. And kept them there. It didn't take long for us to get talking when someone sat us together in the canteen and after that we started messaging each other throughout the day. Last Thursday I gave her a lift home after work and she told me that she spends a lot of her weekends alone, going for walks or finding good places to eat, usually in Richmond. In other words, she doesn't like many people. Same here. I thought this is the one.

Last Friday I said to her what you doing weekend and she said busy tonight and Saturday. I said here's my number, call me any time if you would like to have lunch in Richmond.

I thought that she might call on Sunday, but she didn't.

Back at work on Monday early morning, she walked past purposely not looking at me. I texted her "Boo." No answer. She avoided me all day. Last thing that afternoon, she was sitting alone so I went over to say hello. Completely cold reception.

This *volte face* can only be because she must have read about me over the weekend—my newspaper articles, my book on Amazon. She has gone off me either because she found out I lost my kids and she thinks I'm trouble or, much more likely I think, because she found out my age.

Being over forty is like having leprosy.

72

As for Beth, we arrived in the building simultaneously this morning and she tried to run up the stairs "not" seeing me but I said in loud cheerful voice "Hi Beth, how are you today!"

She's gone back to giving me the eye again. Women!

73

Today I had arranged to go lunch with my new GSK mate Ian, who sits next to Beth, so I texted him "invite Beth." Surprisingly she actually joined us. At the canteen table, she wouldn't look at me, faced sideways on to Ian, and answered anything I said to Ian!

She's young. I guess she's very shy and she knows she has been blanking me all week, so literally "couldn't face me."

I meet young women all the time, either by going out or befriending barmaids and waitresses, whose phone numbers make up half the people on my phone book, and they're all true friends in that I have gone out with them and done stuff with them on a weekly basis for over a year each. I like young women's company.

74

Every time I tell my mum and brothers about the latest twenty-something female they make me feel like Gary Glitter. I am open that I like young women and I accept that they see me as old. Same as when I was young, I didn't know anyone more than about two years senior to me, apart from a quantum leap to my Dad's peers, who were more like Olympians than contemporaries.

75

Actually met a woman my own age last night (well close). First time since 1994, when I met my wife. During the last couple years it's been a string of twenty-year-olds messing me around. Anyway this new paramour said last night let's have dinner tonight. I texted her to that effect this afternoon, and called her half an hour ago. No answer. Prefer to be messed around by the younger models.

76

The Times (I'm now reading in Maids café)—which ought to and does know better, but telling the truth is not the mission of newspapers—proclaims on today's front page "Ebola on Same Scale as AIDS Epidemic." Let's see—four thousand dead from Ebola. According to Wikipedia, thirty-five million AIDS deaths to date and a further thirty-five million infected.

77

I had a good dream this morning. I was strolling near a farm and a bull with horns was straining at a fence. I said look at that bull protecting his cows. Then the bull got out and confronted me. I tried to push it back. I went to the farmhouse to report the escaped bull. I knew that the farmer was the farmer who lived at the neighboring farm when I was a kid, Mick Curle. That was it.

This dream is about work as represented by Mick Curle, a model entrepreneur when I was a kid. He built his own business as I am doing now. The bull is a manifestation of someone's jealousy—someone who was thinking about me this morning. I think I know who it is—the chief investigator on a GSK clinical study I'm reporting. He's jealous for a few reasons, mainly in that I drafted the research article whereas he can't. I finished that bit of writing yesterday; could it be possible that the news leaked somehow? We are psychic creatures.

78

Back to Beth. She pretty much snubbed me all week in that I didn't get any chance to speak to her and when I said hello to her she said hi then instantly looked away both times. Gone are the naughty looks she used to give me as well. Then this afternoon, when I was off guard, she gave me such a smile.

79

I was out till 4 a.m. last night, just woke up. I looked at my phone and saw a new app [Snapchat] which I must have downloaded last night. On it are pics and videos of myself with some girls I met last night. I had totally forgotten but the reminders brought them back. The videos showed *their* last night, starting with their getting ready to go out earlier, I guess. Running around with their tits out. Crazy app. What do I do on Friday nights? On the app I saw videos that I got a taxi home with those young girls. Now I remember, they live round the corner. Loneliness is driving me mad. I also had a vivid dream last night. I was in a Milton Keynes-style shopping mall, and a golden retriever pup slowly walked up to me, so I adopted it. We ambled about through the crowds of shoppers, possibly looking for the doggie's owner. That was all. The dog was the same dog I petted in a pub early last night. The dog in the dream was Beth the girl who has been driving me nuts at GSK. I just know it. The dream means, I am hard to understand, but I want you to take me.

80

Something else happened yesterday which also could be connected to my being the oldest teenager in town. I was cycling across Trafalgar Square when I found myself amid three scruffy youths also on bikes, one of whom maneuvered in front of me then braked, causing me to mutter something. Then they caught up with me and one of them crashed into the back of my bike—just tire to tire—and said in a sarcastic voice "Sorry." It was quite unreal. They were kids, teens or early twenties. I then carried on going and again, one of them rode alongside me in "accidental" near collision, so I said angrily "What's the matter?" This seemed to wake him up that I was senior (the way his face changed) and he cycled off fast, and that was it.

December, 2014

81

I'm sitting in a good Thai restaurant now and ensconced nearby are some very obese Asians (look Indian) really relishing their food. Maybe the greatest pleasures for humans are food, rest, and sex. Only westerners invented philosophy and an idea that adventure is a thrill. No other humans leapt to those conclusions.

82

I could say fuck it and go down the pub and drink all day, who'd care? I described an all-day piss-up in my book you read recently (about one day I spent in Zürich) and since that one-off, years ago, I only have had one other all-day drinking bout, also years ago, when my "wife" kicked me out the house, a few months before she kidnapped my two beautiful daughters, whom I never saw again.

That day I went to the pub, and remember sitting in the local park at one point, very pissed. A homeless man, literally. I lost everything, but I survived to tell the tale. No one you or I know lost everything as I did. We both have lost parents, but that is natural. Losing your kids is unnatural, and the pain lasts forever.

Happy Christmas!

London, January 2015

83

In Memory of Ernie Boucher

I was just recalling that my personal tutor at Sussex (the person you go to with any problems) was Harry Kroto, Nobel Prize winner in chemistry, as I occasionally tell anyone who might be interested. Then I remembered that actually Kroto was my second personal tutor. You are only supposed to have one personal tutor throughout uni, but my original PT, Ernie Boucher, died. He might have committed suicide—he was found washed up on the shore at Brighton, or so I heard. Boucher was brilliant. A maverick with much integrity—such people will always be remembered fondly. He used to digress brilliantly during lectures. Half the students walked out in a huff but I was enthralled. One time he walked over to the window (during a digression), looked out at the sunny green campus, and said, "What are you young people doing in here? You should be out there, making love!" (Or something like that.) Many students did go out there—but not to make love, in anger. Boucher was the only scientist I heard point out that the ice crystal collapses on melting—unlike all other compounds, water is denser in liquid than in solid phase. This, he speculated, means that if the world's ice fields were to melt, due to global warming, then the water level must go down, not up. He had a parasitic disease, picked up in Mexico he told me. Nothing visible on the outside, but he was dying inside. That might have been why he committed suicide. How little do nineteen year olds know about what troubles middle-aged men and women. I thought I should write something about Ernie Boucher, before he is forgotten.

84

Drearily predictable. The BBC almost immediately yesterday wheeled out a "counterterrorism expert" and fired at him a bunch of loaded questions designed to make him say the U.K. is at risk. How can anyone swallow this shit—and everyone does. I just don't need to hear any of it [news], it gives me nightmares. I would rather concentrate on how to have an enjoyable life.

March 2015

85

I take a walk on this heath every day. On this land, I have closely observed the seasons change since late summer last year.

86

Just witnessed [at a GSK corporate event] a mind-numbing set of presentations from people who have gone mad. What has the western world come to? In all earnestness these grinning salaried twerps reiterated "our people" "our values" "our culture" "our vision" etc. etc. etc. for over ninety minutes. Hasn't that kind of talk become a joke yet? Obviously not. During the discussions, I realized what these people sound like—born-again Christians delivering a self-assured, self-righteous sermon. Except they don't believe in anything spiritual beyond selling products. A spiritual null in which we live, among people who have no soul.

87

Here's some amusing nonsense about Beth (remember her?—girl at my work who hasn't spoken to me directly for half a year now). We still have this thing where she ignores me and I in return pretend not to notice her, then we catch each other looking. It's a game and it's not just my imagination. Anyway my story. My car failed M.O.T. [U.K. safety certificate] so I'm on the train this week. On Monday morning I sat towards the back of the train because the entrance to my local station (where I just wait on platform) is that end. When I got off at my stop and shuffled out with the crowd, I saw Beth coming from the front of the train. I thought "Beth sits in the front each day." We've all got our habits. The following day I sat in the front hoping to see her or have a chance to say hello. She wasn't on it, but there was an early corporate event that day (which I told you about) and she was already at GSK when I arrived. The next day (Wednesday), the train was canceled. So today was my next chance "accidentally" to be in Beth's carriage. Guess what—I didn't see her till I jumped out at the destination—and she exited from the back of the train! I wonder—did she go there to "bump into" me, supposing I always sit at the back?

88

One massive source of confusion for males is their not understanding that feeling beautiful is the number one important thing for women. Listen to the chatter of two women—it is endlessly about cosmetic products and especially things that uplift their appearance—clothes and handbags. Women are obsessed with their looks. As soon as they sit down they get out a mirror and do their makeup. When they stand up they check their reflection in the window. And to get confirmation that they are attractive they like to make sure that men are noticing them. I think that is the main reason women exchange looks—pick a man they fancy and keep him looking their way by flashing him looks. However, the man thinks that she genuinely desires him when really all she requires is her own self-assurance that she's attractive. This is why girls who have a boyfriend even sitting right next to them will still exchange looks with other guys. And it is also why a man who gets sufficient looks to make an approach often gets shocked by the cold shoulder he receives for his trouble.

89

Strange nightmare last night (most of my dreams are probably nightmares). I was at my Dad's place in Tinkers Bridge [Milton Keynes, U.K.]. At night. There was some preliminary action which I forget now, but could remember well last night when I awoke from the nightmare. In it, I was in the upstairs bedroom with my brother Chris when the blanket we were sitting under started thrashing around. We were both paralyzed. This is something that I have experienced many times while awake on the border of sleep, and seems to me a recurrent nexus of the transition between the waking and sleeping worlds—the blanket tearing off or struggling. Perhaps the blanket, symbolic of sleep, and the movement, emblematic of waking, are struggling together. Anyway back to the dream, the blanket started jumping around and my brother and I were paralyzed, then in the corner of the room appeared a black ghost. It had the appearance of a *Planet of the Apes* ape. I tried to point at it and say to Chris what's that, but I was paralyzed. Then (in the dream) I awoke, or that part of the dream was over. My Dad appeared and I told him that until we agree with the ghost not to enter that room again, it will continue to appear. My Dad was mocking me that there is no such thing as ghosts. Then he turned into a Tyrannosaurus, although was still my Dad, talking and telling me not to believe in ghosts. Finally, the strangest part! My brother and I decided to leave the haunted house and just as we walked out the door, my daughters Selene and Cale said they wanted to come with us—except in the dream they were the living, 3-D embodiments of Gainsborough's paintings of his two daughters in the National Gallery (the girls in the paintings—complete with eighteenth century dress).

This dream was inspired principally by my being off work yesterday and thinking that I'd be going back to work today. I was thinking that once again I'd be surrounded by a bunch of corporate scientists and their obsessions with buying products and what's on TV. By being uninterested in what interests most other people, I have basically dropped out of society. The dream was my belief in spirituality and that there is more in the world than can be explained by science— the supernatural. Indeed, my Dad who told me there is no such thing as spirits then turned into a dinosaur—nice representation of someone whose (to me) old-fashioned views (a total belief in rationality / reality) are out of touch with my own views, which have moved beyond an atheistic belief in science, which I think holds back the western world today. Also, the ghost was a *Planet of the Apes* ghost, suggestive of the future of humanity transformed into *Planet of the Apes* humans. As for my girls being Gainsborough's daughters, the girls in the painting are truly the spitting images of Selene and Cale when they were five and three, and yesterday I walked back from Richmond to Kew via Sheen, and in so doing passed my accountant's office (Gainsborough House) and walked up Gainsborough Road, so was thinking of Gainsborough and the painter's connection to me via our lookalike daughters.

90

Here's some nonsense cos I haven't written for a while and I'm bored! It's about Beth, so if you don't wanna know, don't bother reading! For the last two weeks she and I went through exaggerated levels of ignoring each other. For example, if I saw her approaching down a corridor, I would slip into an anteroom till she went past. Then last Friday, I overheard her talking to her female friend / colleague. They went into a whisper, even though I was the only person nearby. I just-heard "How tall is he?" "Six foot" "I'd better wear flat shoes." Her friend was trying to hook-up Beth with someone. Although I pretended I didn't care, actually I did. Her friend asked Beth, "You are coming on Sunday aren't you?" She replied "Yes if it's sunny." As I listened I thought, she doesn't really want to meet this guy. Over the weekend I was in pain. I was actually relieved that the weather was bad on Sunday. I thought "She won't go." On Monday (yesterday), back in the office I heard Beth's friend ask her, "So what did you do at the weekend?" It means they didn't meet, I guess. All day on Monday Beth batted her eyes at me. She kept turning around and staring. She is aware of me all the time (and I her, naturally), and her behavior on Monday was because of this intruder, in whom she has no interest. I'll summarize what goes on between us like this. If you had a nightmare neighbor, all the noise and confrontations would be very real and ongoing for you, but you alone. Nobody else would really be able to feel how much this annoyance intrudes on your everyday life. And my ongoing drama with Beth is the same— only we (or maybe only I) know it, no one else perceives it. It's only a big deal to me. She's sitting opposite me now, determined to ignore me. Her behavior of the last few days must be because of this other person, and now she's restored my interest (my agony), it's back to the old game.

91

A.R.: Did you message her?

Looks like I didn't, luckily. I bumped into her [Beth] at the entrance to GSK this morning and she scowled at me, as usual.

92

As you know I've been chronically sex starved for years. Really, throughout my thirties and forties so far. When you are single, sex starved, and earning a lot of money it doesn't take you long to investigate escorts. I did (online). Prices were over £150. I thought no thanks, not in London. I'd rather go to a proper European red light district where what you see is what you get.

Last Friday [in Brussels], I said to myself "Tonight I'm going to sit in a lively bar and see if I can pick up a Belgian lass. If not, tomorrow I'm going to pay for a lay." Nothing happened on the Friday night. At one point two beautiful young girls spoke to me in French. I said, um my French is pretty atrocious. They then talked and laughed with the barman and didn't look at me again. It made up my mind.

I'm now going to paint four portraits.

On Saturday I went to the red light district near Brussels Noord station. It's a seedy street with girls sitting in windows. Lowlife men, the dregs of society, worker types, trawled up and down. Needless to say I knew that I was the same. At least the girls banged on their windows and beckoned me, unlike at the other men. So I must have looked somewhat different.

I couldn't do it. It was too sordid. I went into the station to catch a train to Antwerp. As I got to the platform and pressed the door-open button on the carriage, the door stayed closed and the train departed. I had a half-hour wait for the next one.

I went back and looked for the only pretty girl I had seen earlier. I went up to her window and mouthed how much? She smiled and held up four fingers. I didn't know whether that was forty or four hundred. I went inside and she was super friendly. Forty euros for a fuck or fifty with positions. It was surreal. I was shaking with nervousness. Okay I'll skip the next twenty minutes. She simply took off what little clothes she was wearing and lay on the bed.

After we finished, she put her bikini back on and walked out the room. She had been fun to talk to and gave me a great time, but that was a shock. I thought, this is her work. I got dressed and followed her out, and was pleasantly surprised that she was waiting for me at the door, and gave me a peck per cheek as I left.

I was intrigued. On the one hand it was really unerotic, on the other strangely compelling. When I arrived in Antwerp, I went straight to the city's red light district. I had rushed and panicked on my first tryst, and this time I wanted to be a bit more fastidious. At the red light district, I looked at all the girls left and right. Once again they seemed to like me more than the other low-lives! I turned a corner and there she was. Blonde, beautiful (not tarty beautiful, really beautiful), in red suspenders standing in her window beaming at me. I asked her how much. Forty euros.

I'll skip the next twenty minutes except to say this smart, funny, super-intelligent girl left me thinking that was the best s** I've ever had. Her *derrière* was a masterpiece. Her walk, her sultry demeanor, her everything. A real blonde from Romania.

The next day (yesterday) I went back to Brussels and like the debauch I have become (temporarily, no more after this) was soon strolling down my familiar street. This time I made a mistake. I caught sight of a pair of pretty eyes and went over to the girl while she was attending to something in her little display window, and when she looked up and smiled me in I thought she was not so attractive, with a big bum and slightly protruding belly but at the age these girls are, she was firm and fit. Inside her boudoir, as I waited for her to go hide the money somewhere, I honestly felt that I didn't want to screw her. Needless to say, she changed my mind pretty quick when she returned. This one also walked out after we (I) finished, and this was horrible, when I dressed and followed her out the little bedroom, she was back in her window and waving her bum at someone outside! She gave me the obligatory peck on the cheek though.

This morning, I thought, last one. Girl number three had been so stupid and empty and provided such a perfunctory experience, I didn't learn anything from her. So I returned to Brussels Gare Du Nord for the last time. As I walked up the red light street, one girl was not sitting in her window but rather inside a room that had a window, so she seemed detached. I walked past several more girls blowing me kisses and wiggling their bums, then went back to this other girl, who like the ones before was sweet, smiled, made me feel as though she liked what she does. Skip the next twenty minutes. After, she lay on my shoulder and we talked like a couple, about this and that. She kissed me and although our saliva did not get exchanged the corner of her mouth stopped a millimeter from mine. She said I was good and I believe her. She asked me did I want her to accompany me for the rest of the day and she gave me her phone number when I left.

As I prepare to return to my normal daily routine, this experiment is over. I learned that prostitutes, at least in Belgium, are warm, sexy creatures, interesting figures, the one in Antwerp was by all means a perfectly beautiful, smart girl, a girl who could marry any millionaire, hospitable women and wonderful company.

Tomorrow, I shall continue my search to find a partner, to whom I will love and devote myself.

93

A.R.: Bloody hell… coke! You're losing the plot. Coke FFS! And you mention it in such a casual way too. This is tragic. Rather you than me. I've never touched drugs in my life.

Then in that case, you are unable to make a comment. I agree with Terence McKenna, that because every new drug since the 1950s (e.g. LSD) is immediately suppressed by all governments, there have been no dose-finding studies equivalent to those used in pharmaceutical industry and so safe limits have not been established. It's nonsense to say that drugs are simply dangerous, otherwise all those present last Saturday would not be back to normal at work now (we are). Clearly, drugs are also enjoyable, which is why they have always been sought. Obviously, it is not a good idea for a father of teenage kids (you) to be getting out of his face, so I can understand why these agents are not appropriate for you. But for someone who has nothing better to do, ever (me), why not (occasionally)? I don't have any further plans to do it again any time soon. By the way, only myself and one other, later joined by a third person, participated. Three others who were there didn't join in. It was not "a mad night with young people all going crazy"—just sitting around at the home of one of them. Terence McKenna was also right to argue that the suppression of drugs and their proclamation, as widely disseminated in the tool of the powers-that-be, the news media, that these compounds are dangerous, are also part of the same mind control perpetrated on members of society everywhere. What better definition of mind control can there be than not allowing people to alter their minds, even briefly?

May 2015

94

A.R.: I'll be fifty years old in a couple of weeks and it's bearing down on me.

Why? You can openly say you are fifty years old. Because everyone you know, knows you. There is not one person in my world to whom I can happily admit my age (although everyone surely can guess). It's my guilty secret. Why? Because after I lost everything, I had to compete to survive again. I did not put my date of birth on my CV in order to get a role at GSK, thinking if I revealed my age I'd be unemployable.

You're a father of three boys who must be all coming up to twenty. I'm not. That makes you fifty. It makes me a renegade.

Tomorrow I enter the final third of my forties.

95

Here are some of the quotes I was supposed to feel sorry for recently (all genuine):

"I can't believe I'm twenty-two"—J.T.
"I can't afford motor insurance until I'm twenty-five"—R.F.

"Shit I'm gonna be thirty next year"—A.K.

96

I haven't burthened you with one of my dreams for a while, so here's one from last night!

I was in a community, maybe it was San Francisco, and all the people were sweating blood. They had blood all over their faces and seeping through their clothes. Just a thin amount. I did as well. We were all saying that we sweated blood. It seemed a normal thing. Then we were near an airport, and a bunch of passengers from New York arrived and came out through the exits. They did not sweat blood. I gathered that in New York, people did not sweat blood. Then (I was with a female companion), we were going through the gates toward our flight bound for New York, and I said to her, "Where's your blood? You are not sweating blood anymore." She replied "I don't sweat blood." Then I saw that I didn't either. Then my alarm woke me up.

This dream is to do with my recent depression and loneliness. I was even thinking yesterday, if I died at home after drinking, how long would it be till I were found? Silly thoughts. The dream expressed this. Blood is clearly about morbidity. My being covered in blood symbolizes disease and weariness. But the people of New York carried on regardless of how I feel. As did the people of San Francisco eventually. The dream meant my little problems are nothing to anybody else, so get over them. The dream was probably also inspired by, yesterday, the people in my department [at GSK] were talking about going to the pub, and indeed, at four o'clock, they all went, all of them, without me. No one said a word to me. I was quite flabbergasted that my department would arrange (in advance, because some of them who normally drive came in by train in the morning), would all go to the pub without mentioning a word to me (about a dozen of us all sit around two long tables). So the dream also meant that regardless of how lonely and left out I feel, the rest of the world would just carry on without me, without a care. Their indifference to me is nothing personal—I simply don't matter to them. I just have to get on with it.

97

In a pub in Richmond now, [The Jam's] "In The City" just came on the speaker, knocked me sideways. Punk, so real, so young, was so unlike the '80s pop charts and metal.

98

A.R.: Fuck it! This time next week I'll be fifty!

Congratulations! That's all. You did it. Yes it is an achievement, unlike being young.

I once read a psychiatry book in which all the mental characteristics of people in different age groups were classified, and the oldest (over eighties) only had two types: contentment... or despair. Yes, no other personality trait was presented after that age.

I'm going to try to make sure I'm in the first group, and that starts now.

99

Things happen for a reason but I'm stumped by this one.

Last night I went out to eat, sat down, and noticed Ray across the dining-room. With his white hair and blue suit, you can't miss him. Then I couldn't believe my eyes. He was accompanied with a woman I dated for a few weeks last year. She looked stunning. She's about thirty, he's about seventy (but in great nick for a rich wino). I can't think how they met. She lives and works in Kingston. Ray, as far as I can tell, never leaves Kew (I mean he's in the Coach & Horses pub twenty-four hours a day).

I ran out. Outside, I stopped to text my mate Joe (who knows Ray as well). While I was tapping my phone, Ray stepped outside for a cigarette. I said I know your companion in there. Ray said yes, she told me she knows you. I said eh? Why did

I come up in conversation? (I don't think she saw me in the restaurant.) Ray was a bit vague (couldn't remember). He uttered that this is only the second time he met her. That suggests he met her once, got her number, and that was their first date. She probably told Ray that she used to go out with a man from Kew, and between them they worked out it was me. In fact, because Ray is a musician from Kew, she must have mentioned me. There can't be too many Alex-s in a band in Kew.

I really can't think why I was presented with that sign. Is it about age difference? I've been thinking recently to give up wishing that I will ever find another girlfriend.

100

A leaving card for me to sign came round the office this afternoon. For Beth. I said I don't think Beth really wants to hear from me. She won't even say hello to me. Then I added, when's she leaving? Friday.

It has really upset me. Hours later, I'm still reeling and sad.

We had an understanding between us, that was unnameable.

Fifteen minutes after I heard she's leaving GSK, I went to look for one of the researchers (for a work reason). I entered a room, and there was Beth sitting alone. We looked at each other—a rare occurrence—in such a way.

101

Beth has been sitting in another location [different building on GSK campus] all this week so there is a chance I won't see her again. She may just fizzle away.

I might have brought this up previously in a similar context. There is a Ray Bradbury story about an alien kept in a glass aquarium with another species of alien kept in another nearby. This first alien falls in love with the other alien and longs to be in the same tank. Years go by and things happen in the lab, and the alien always yearns to be with the other alien. At last the alien is put in the same tank as the other alien, which immediately devours him / it.

You can see how this story might relate to my feelings for Beth!

102

I'm probably a sad, deluded old has-been (which I have acknowledged all along), but the following just happened. I saw Beth in the canteen who gave me an enigmatic smile (in a roundabout way—looked down and smiled briefly). So I messaged her (on GSK internal thing) "This your last day? Good luck." No answer. Those few minutes encapsulated the entire "affair" whereby she wants, and fully encourages, me to fall for her whereas she will not even talk to me. It's something that only we know. I don't know whether she does it to anybody else as well, but I doubt it. She is all corporate with everyone else as far as I can tell.

What can I do though? If she wanted to speak to me she'd have responded to my text earlier. Prior to her hating me (for the first one week only), we texted all day long, so I know she's inclined to do it.

Oh well. In a future date I'll remember her in the same way as all the other Helens who tormented me over the years, just a faded memory that no longer matters.

July 2015

103

Did you ever read Yeats' *Stories of Red Hanrahan*? (My Golden Book). This was the principal reason I went to Ireland (on the Yeats trail).

Red Hanrahan—my single most cherished book ever—starts with the scholar and poet as a young schoolteacher, who on Samhain night is accosted by the Sidhe (faeries) while making his way toward his love, whom he never sees again. This mystical masterpiece spellbound me twenty years ago and mesmerized me even more when I read it once again recently. Towards the end of the saga, Hanrahan sees a young girl crying by the road and when he asks her why, she replies, "I am to be married to so-and-so, who is as old as you are!" Hanrahan is caught off guard and then realizes for the first time that he is old. He composes a Curse of the Old Men and teaches it to all the children, who go around singing it.

A few nights ago in Sligo, not far from Yeats' grave and under the shadow of Knocknarea (feature of Yeats' stories), I was in the pub chatting up a girl of about early thirties I'd say, when she mentioned (out the blue) that I was old. I don't usually get this. She wasn't that young either (compared with some of the girls I've been out with lately). I replied maybe I just appear older than you are. She replied, no you are old. It was my Red Hanrahan moment and had to happen during that trip.

104

Dear Zac Goldsmith—This is a follow-up to our correspondences last year regarding the abduction in Japan of my two children five years ago.

I am sure you will remember this issue.

Last year, after a six-month wait, the Foreign Office responded to our inquiries as to what the U.K. government is prepared to do about my and many other British children's abduction in Japan, by sending me a list of lawyers who can speak English in Japan.

Does the U.K. government think I am so stupid that I never thought of that?

I have long suspected that the U.K. government would rather have British citizens abducted than say anything against Japan (and Japan's trade / military presence in Asia, etc.).

Here is a brief summary of what happened to my children.

April 2010: My wife suddenly moved to an apartment with our two small children. To fund this, she stole [withdrew from bank] approximately $300,000 of family savings. Because I had to pay the family mortgage and support myself, I had to continue working. This meant while I was occupied, my children were escorted to and from school each day then kept inside my wife's apartment every night and at weekends. I never saw, apart from glimpses, or spoke to my children again.

2010–11: I attended "Family Court" in Japan. This fruitless mediation consisted of a separate visit made by my wife and then myself to court "mediators" who listened to my wife's demands and then my pleas, and merely recounted them to each party. During mediation, the court never made any of its own decisions. Finally, after eighteen months of the same, a judge decided that I should pay my wife a nominal monthly amount of upkeep ($300) in return for one visit to see my children in a public place as agreed with my wife per month. This ruling was not enforceable, my wife ignored it, and I still never saw my children. I reported this to the court, which took no further action.

April 2012: I lost my job in a Japanese medical publishing house after twelve years' service due to "cost cutting." Because I could not find any similar work, I had to move out my house in order to rent it to a tenant to pay the mortgage. Depressed, fed up, and facing teaching English for peanuts and living in a shack in the outskirts of Tokyo (all that I would be able to afford), I emigrated first to the U.S. (where my Mom and brothers live) and then finally to Richmond where I currently reside.

On subsequent visits to Japan, my attempts to see and talk to my children as they walked to and from school resulted in my arrest by the local police and warning not to go near my two children.

Without any legal framework my wife abducted my two children who adored their loving daddy. My wife is protected by her community including neighbors I don't even know, who will interfere with my approaching my children.

Now I want my MP to speak out about this in the U.K. Houses of Parliament. I want it stated that Japanese people have *carte blanche* to abduct British minors. I want it recognized that the concept of a family differs in Japan from other advanced nations and that due to this cultural difference a Japanese person can take children away from the other parent with the assistance of Japanese authorities (family court, police, children's school). I want it known that Japanese people can, and do, steal and lie to children and do not think it essential that a child can meet his or her loving other parent. The Japanese are people who send fathers of children to work abroad, alone, for periods of years. The Japanese are people who work employees to death (it is called *karoushi*) and no one does anything to change that. They are culturally chasms apart from British values and I say it is the duty of the British government to acknowledge this so as to warn British nationals who live / work / marry / have children in Japan that their and their children's human rights are at risk of arbitrary violation.

Thank you for your kind attention.

Dear Mr Kahney—As discussed, Zac [Goldsmith, MP for Richmond Park] contacted the Foreign Office on your behalf, to ask what further avenues of support and assistance were open to you, and Minister of State, Hugo Swire MP, has issued the attached response [enclosed a list of lawyers in Japan]. Should you require Zac's support or help in anyway, please don't hesitate to get back in touch.

Dear Zac—Thank you for your recent efforts on my behalf and response from Hugo Swire MP [who sent a list of lawyers]. Needless to say, the response although sympathetic is inadequate. No one, either inadvertently or purposely, is listening to my message. In Japan there is no legal recourse.

Japanese children are raised by schools. Their fathers have little to do with them. They work all day till late at night. Japanese do not take family holidays, eat out as a family, do anything as a family. I lived in Japan for twelve years and witnessed this. Japanese culture is devised so that children spend their lives at school (till late night) and at the end, they join a company and begin a life of overwork. If you do not fit in with this life, as I increasingly rejected and wanted to take my wife and children out, you might find yourself rejected from that system and kept out. That is what happened to me.

Zac you asked me whether there is anything more that you could do and the answer is yes. You yourself or your team could research child abduction in Japan. Child abduction occurs all over the world but that in Japan is unique in that the losing parent is an educated, hard-working, productive parent. Indeed, a requirement of gaining a working visa in Japan is a university education. Child abduction in Japan has a constant pattern in that the losing parent does not want to become a round-the-clock worker and (in my case) wishes to leave Japan. After I lost my children I joined many "left-behind parent" groups and met many, many other LBPs and we all have a similar story. The Japanese child abductor wants the children to learn Japanese culture and that means growing up in Japan. She / he is surrounded by like-minded people who believe inherently that the best thing for the children of a Japanese mother is for the children to be raised by the mother and by schools (which dictate every aspect of the child's life, including weekends, in terms of what the child eats, wears, comports herself, speaks, the lot) and that a father has no right to interfere. A father works and provides money.

OK I don't want to keep repeating myself.

What I would entreat you to do is look into this or have someone in your office research child abduction in Japan (numbers, outcome, legal recourse, etc.). If you become convinced, I would like this raised in the U.K. House of Commons along the following lines (I know we do not judge other cultures). How is it that a modern democracy, ally, and trade partner with extensive links to the U.K. and broader world has no equipment to resolve and enforce joint custody following parental separation (which is as common in Japan as elsewhere)? How is it that the many (thousands) of Britons who live, work, and marry in Japan are offered no legal protection in their adoptive country? As we have seen, Britons (and countless other nationals especially Americans) are losing their children with new victims coming forward day by day.

What can be done to protect U.K. citizens and their children in future? Many thousands are at risk of this human rights violation. It seems that pressure on Japan to update their society is needed, if that country wishes to be on the world stage. The way to cajole any country to cooperate is diplomatic pressure and, failing that, sanctions. Japan is a rock in the Pacific with no resources and needs to import every raw material. Japan is extremely vulnerable to sanctions.

The above is my proposal. I am not a politician and I do not know how parliament works but this is going to affect more and more British nationals. It is not going to go away. Please look into this on behalf of your constituent.

[No further reply from Zac Goldsmith's office]

105

I just received a GSK corporate e-mail that contained the following sentence and other similar ones:

> "This is in preparation for the new company (GB67) becoming transactional after business cutover on 3 August in GB&I and the following entities will be impacted."

I have no idea what it means. The e-mail also included a snapshot of a gloating female consumer in the setting of a corporate HQ.

I have less than one percent connection with this world.

106

I avoid TV like the plague, but just caught wind of some drivel while walking past one of the TVs continually broadcasting BBC news here at GSK. It was an item about new smartphones from China. As always when talking "business," lots of percentages were flashed on the screen ("12.4%" "+18.6% up from Q2") and so on. To ram home the message to the hungry TV audience of consumers, the BBC rolled out a slick be-suited "market trends analyst" to spout a load of talk about the smartphones forecast. It occurred to me: when phones were a dial-up with curly-wire receiver connected to the wall, did anyone know who manufactured those? All the same manufacturer? Myriad manufacturers? I have no idea who used to make household phones.

Another thing I incidentally noted was the death of poor old Whitney Houston's daughter. Family curse there. I suspect she was murdered, although the TV hasn't mentioned anything like that. It's not on their agenda.

The constant TV news personality is a man in a suit with the regulation short-all-over, neat haircut aged about thirty-five-to-forty and talking confidently with lightning responses that are bang-on predictions of how money dominates all. Not too young to be ignored nor too old to be ignored either. Where do they come from? Scripted actors? Where do "political commentators" live? They must be journalists. How can anyone swallow their shit.

August 2015

107

It's one thing to feel sorry for a moment and then forget, and another to grieve forever.

108

Get this. Remember that girl I said we saw each other and smiled at two different locations several hours apart on the same day a few months ago, and you said I would never have a chance to see her again? Well actually I have seen her many times cos she walks the same opposite route to me most lunchtimes and we always smile or say hi when we pass. Yesterday I plucked up courage and spoke to her "Where is it you go every day?" We got talking and I learned a few bits about her.

That was yesterday. Guess what? Today as we passed (I was conversing on my phone) I saw that she was fully made up! Usually she has the plain office look but today she appeared like she was going on a night out! I'm sure it was for our meeting today. Sadly I couldn't stop so gave her just a wave but tomorrow I'll definitely talk to her.

109

At lunchtime today I perambulated down my usual walkabout deliberately *sans* my phone. The "girl" (still don't know her name) was a bit late so when I spotted her she was strolling towards me on the other side of the road to our usual side. But, as we drew close she crossed to my side seemingly to invite a conversation. I said hi, you going to work? "Yes." I don't get it, do you start work at twelve? "Yes, I have two jobs, one in the morning and then this one at Sony in the afternoon." I said, it's funny, we walk past each other every day, I wish I could talk to you more. For instance, at Sony, do you work with Japanese people? Do you speak Japanese? I lived in Japan for a while.

She smiled and started moving towards work, seemingly because late (the conversation was actually a bit longer than the above), so I said is there a number I can text you on? She laughed (smiled) and said I'll see you next week!

I would take that as a no, except one thing: Why did she cross the road to come and talk to me?

I will never, ever understand women.

A.R.: She won't be interested in a fifty year old if she's under thirty. That's a fact!

...except I'm not fifty, you are.

She looks about thirtyish. I'm sick of this. Our friends the newspaper and TV people are fervently anti-age gap in relationships, for the usual reasons (control of people), and so there are regular attacks on such goings-on, where the older man is depicted as debauched and scandalous. I saw one news report the other day; it was a red carpet awards thing where [actress / pop singer] Selene Gomez (described as twenty-three) was pictured with her two male co-stars from her latest movie. They were aged around forties and dressed like slobs and she was wearing a glittering dress, and the article described how "uncomfortable" she was, appearing next to two older men, who "should know better" etc., etc., etc. Actually, she looked relaxed, I bet they know and get on with each other well while on set. The news media are anti-anything that does not conform to their normality, which they themselves create to foist down the people's necks. Every day you will see a "sex scandal"-type story in the news, featuring an over-forty man.

During the last two years, I have gone out for a meal / drinks with at least ten, maybe more, younger women, I am discreet, no one pays us any attention, there's nothing dirty or sordid about it, there's nothing dirty or sordid about me. I'm the same *moi* I have always been, a bit older, that's all. If anyone tells me I am not a good potential partner for anyone I say I'm intelligent, a writer and musician, unattached, well presented, well read, educated, got my own company, mind your own business.

The news is replete with double standards. On the one hand all "old perverts" are villainized where possible whereas on the other the news glorifies young girls while ostensibly pretending to be uninterested. Any girl showing a bit of tit or leg can get her pic in the news. A few years ago there was a headline declaring (bragging) "Rolling Stone Mick Cheats on Wife with Fifteen-Year-Old Girl." If it were not Mick Jagger and instead a politician or teacher, the headline would have been "Sick Pervert Brought to Justice for Molesting Schoolgirl!"

Why the duplicity? Same reason as always, to control and bring down the populace. Celebs are allowed to get away with anything. Why? Because they are created as a fantasy for the people-slaves to wish they could commingle. Celebs possess everything but the news media strictly separates their lives from ours. We are normal, they are not. Why not? Because it is subconsciously suggested in our heads that we can never have a good life. Only those lucky ones can do as they please, not us.

Open any newspaper and see how women are represented, and then contrast that with all the daily attacks on old perverts.

This world is controlled by immensely wealthy people who require everyone to exist far below them so as to validate their wealth. Everyone works for these controllers.

110

I've long maintained that the purpose of television / news is to rob you of your aspirations and it does so in very subtle ways. The *only* method not to be sucked (suckered) into it is not to watch it.

111

Because of the shitty town where I grew up in the violent Eighties, even now when I see a bloke in casual attire coming towards me I expect him to start on me! This happened just a moment ago on Thames River Path. After the bloke (who was just minding his own business) walked past, I went on the alert in case he ran up and attacked me from behind. I'm scarred for life!

112

I might as well clarify rumors of my vanity publications. Someone on Facebook the other day mentioned my last book and added the throwaway line "when you had it published"—this was someone I've never even met! Obviously everyone assumes my books have been vanity publications. My first *published* book (*Tokyo Trilogy*) initially went through the same long, depressing round of rejection as my inaugural effort *Weeks* had done beforehand. This was around 2004 maybe, when I first finished it. I sent the manuscript to a load of publishers and agents in U.K. and U.S. All rejected, at least twenty or more. That's when I gave up, or ninety-five percent gave up. I even had a half-hearted agent in Tokyo, remember him? He was David Peace (successful author)'s agent as well. He (agent) died a few years ago, and I recently found his obituary in *The Guardian* online, written by David Peace (check William Miller literary agent if interested). So that book went on hold for ages, I just forgot about it.

Then a mate of mine in Tokyo published his book of poetry. He got a grant from university to publish it. I went to the launch party at a bar in Tokyo and met Joe the publisher, who remarked I could send him the manuscript for *Tokyo Trilogy*. I did. It went out to a couple reviewers who were associated with the publisher. One of them said reject, and it was. That was it, I thought "Fuck this I give up." That was 2007 or '08. Then, a year later I again met the publisher at another do, and he said he would publish *Tokyo Trilogy* via print on demand. I had to unearth the manuscript and even rewrote the ending, which sorely needed reworking. It was published—fifty or a hundred copies were made, I believe. *Vanity Publication Alert!* After it was published, Joe asked me for $300 to cover the delivery, ISBN number, paper, etc. So that made *Tokyo Trilogy* a vanity publication, because a writer is not supposed to pay anything towards the cost of producing a book. In my defense, I didn't know beforehand and yes, my vanity is so high that I would not have done a vanity publication (too vain to vanity publish).

Two years later, having lost my kids and gone to ruin on every side, literally fallen apart (where I continue to be, right at the bottom of the heap), I wrote my next book, *Life & Nihonjin*, which was actually a collection of old e-mails leading up to my disaster, a (new) account of the disaster itself, and a long essay on my adoptive country of Japan and what might happen to anyone who goes to live there. That also was read and accepted by the same publisher, Joe, who forged it again on print-on-demand without a word of my contributing towards paying anything, and only after it went on sale did he ask me, unexpectedly, to cover the cost of printing. So, two vanity publications although I didn't know that beforehand. I only wanted my book out there (the second one).

For the record, the print copy has not sold anything, or at least the publisher has not notified me of any sales, and I think it has not sold one copy, even to my Mom or any of my family, my account of how I lost my children three years ago and still cannot have any contact with them—my life and joy, gone just like that. My experience of writing three full-length books, a couple short stories, and one *manga* comic has left me in no doubt whatsoever that no one gives a f*** about my story or my writing! I guess the majority of people feel that way about themselves anyway, without having to find out by composing a few books. My writing experience has told me not to bother. I could possibly write a commercial book aimed squarely at not upsetting people or making them laugh or scream, but why would I want to write a book like that?

The following books were not published in their authors' lifetimes, except as vanity pubs or not at all:

> *Leaves of Grass* (vanity)
> Emily Dickinson's poems (not at all)
> Thoreau's *Walden* (vanity)
> Shakespeare's plays (not at all although performed successfully on stage)
> Poe's tales (appeared in newspapers, not compiled as book despite Poe's attempts)

Can't think of any others! Nick Drake was recorded professionally but his records died a death during his lifetime and so did he (die a death). Some books and music are simply before their time!

113

Last night, I took a train home with a girl who can't be much over twenty-one because she inferred that she recently "graduated uni." We had both attended a poetry and music event and I played a few songs, and she read out a poem. After, we were standing outside in the street when I said I was going to catch a train and she said she was going the same way so we walked (quite far) to the station, and when we arrived we had a half-hour wait for the train and then a short journey (for me, I got off first). So, about an hour talking together rounded off with a cuddle. She was interesting and a nice talker of her broad range of experiences. But, I didn't find her really attractive and I didn't flirt with her or show off, just conversed. I hardly even thought about it last night, because I am so used to hanging out with similar people. But carrying on from what we discussed recently, this tells me that I am not just looking for a young lover, but someone I fancy and find compatible. It is regardless of age, although for her to be attractive, she can't be too old (a grannie), for obvious reasons. I meet loads of young women, mostly barmaids and waitresses. That juxtaposition (of customer to waitress) allows me to make jokes and ask for phone numbers, and I keep getting them. These girls are students, ex-students, and adventurous Europeans drawn to London. They are my type. One of them will stick. Once I have a girlfriend / companion, I would like to do all the things I miss: travel, go places, go cinema, stuff I don't want to do alone any more cos I get depressed.

P.S. My only other way to meet women, a dating app on my phone, is useless. Every other day I send a "charm" to a member I'm informed is nearby, mostly good-looking over thirties whom I apparently passed in the street, and not one of them has responded, out of dozens during the last several months since I downloaded the app. I don't have a mid-life crisis at all, I don't feel old at all. I have a can't-find-a-partner crisis.

114

What are you doing today on your bank holiday? I'm sitting in a Kensington café on my own. The anniversary of my Dad's passing today. I remember a poem by Stephen Dobyns, written in his middle age, which contains the words, "My father, my grandfather, how difficult to recall your faces in my memory anymore." It has taken me one hour to get through a glass wine. So listless.

September 2015

115

Every day I eat alone in GSK canteen (no one ever talks to me or says how are you—not one colleague is aware that I went to Helsinki last weekend, but I would have told anyone who's interested). After lunch, I take a stroll around the heath. GSK campus is set amid beautiful woods. The woods are deserted apart from many animals and birds. I almost bumped into a deer last week. I have never seen anyone from GSK on the heath. I am different to other people, but I think my mental health is sounder than theirs. Most people seem permanently distracted by TV, news, and having to work, all the time.

In Helsinki, I was delighted to find one of my favorite paintings. I can never remember the artist's name, nor was aware it is in Helsinki's gallery. The painting is *Wounded Angel* and depicts an angel with her head bandaged, being carried on a stretcher by grim medics. I had thought it was a WWI painting, but actually was wrought just before that war—1903. It forebodes war. It forebodes the twentieth century. We know that the angel can only have been wounded by men on Earth, yet it is men who carry her to hospital. The carriers know that what they have done is wrong. Standing in front of this awe-inspiring masterpiece, tears streamed down my face! I know the painting because it is on the cover of one of my favorite books, very aptly—Reck-Malleczewen's *Diary of a Man in Despair*—a book I have read many times and felt deep empathy for the author.

Not one person at GSK gives a toss about fallen angels, Reck-Malleczewen, or me!

Right back to work.

116

In a Kew restaurant now. Toffs galore. Beautiful, well spoken, long, chestnut-haired girl dominating the next table with clever banter—wearing a Beatles T-shirt. What a dream.

117

What about staring at your phone for some meaning in life?

October 2015

118

I won't send that thing [letter of appeal against my contract termination at GSK]. It got the injustice off my chest just by writing it. I've lost my job anyway. Linda (my manager) wandered over to my desk today then just stood there. I had to say "What's up?" Then she snapped out of it and said oh nothing and walked off. Never done that before. Later, I was peering through the window of a door when suddenly Steve (top dog), who has been hiding from me, appeared so I opened the door for him and said with a smile Hi Steve—he couldn't possibly pretend not to see that!—so he muttered hello. He looked really sad. I think they all know it's a pernicious trick to let me go but it's just down to money I guess.

119

I don't know what to do for another job yet. This [GSK] is a huge organization and most people here, especially the bosses, just want corporate cronies to get things done. They don't care about quality. It's crap here without Beth anyway.

I'm happy regardless of what happens. This time last year, I was a cornered mouse with a gang of cats moving towards me. But I got out.

120

Just woke up having passed out earlier—and noted that it is still only 9 p.m. I met my mate from Japan Kaz earlier and we started drinking at one o'clock. Couldn't take any more round about six, decamped for home, and must have fallen asleep. Was kinda hoping it were 9 a.m. (Sunday) now, not still early on Saturday night. Might have to get up and go to the pub. What I had thought was a twelve-hour sleep was only about two hours and now I'm fully awake. Thus is the unemployed cycle—excessive nothing time—unless one commits to a project but what? I've already done everything.

121

I drank continually for about thirty-four hours. Started in town on Saturday lunchtime, then I went home and couldn't sleep, so kept drinking all night. Maybe I slept a little in the early hours, but I went to Rock & Rose cocktail bar Sunday around 11 a.m. and continued drinking at home after that. Finally conked out midnight last night. I have no responsibility, literally. I mean, I restrained myself today, but without a work pattern to structure my days (and no one else to look after), I can get pissed whenever I like. I've got nothing better to do. I also know that I am still haunted by my loss of my daughters.

122

I've been on a five-day bender, in Kew / Richmond area. I was waiting for Charlotte at one point, and that was four days ago.

123

The myth of Hercules and the Biblical story of Samson and Delilah both tell of how the great hero lost his strength when his hair was cut off by a woman. Those tales are clearly the same myth with a different hero's name inserted. Why do these ancient traditions both have the same myth of the hero who loses his power when his head is shorn? Long hair is associated with wildness. Short hair is associated with regimented normality and conformity. It is no wonder that rock stars with partying lifestyles grow their hair long. It is no wonder that army recruits and prisoners are issued a crew cut and made to keep their hair short. What is the effect of long hair on a man? A man with long hair has a female quality. He looks unpredictable. He wilfully makes himself look different to other men. Men with short hair tend to look all alike. Long hair is untended. A man with short hair must keep cutting it to keep it short. Short hair is itself work. To keep short hair, a man must watch it. Such attention is the diligence of the conformist. Short hair is conformity. Long hair is rebellion. A long-haired man could suddenly go crazy. A long-haired man doesn't care about keeping up appearances. Long hair is free!

124

Did you watch that program on YouTube about Graham Hancock, talking of how humanity has lost something monumental in its soul...? I do not subscribe to that view. I say that nothing has ever changed. There has always been a mass rabble of humans who care for nothing except filling their faces with food and joining in denouncements of their neighbors, follow latest vogues, and consume what information they are fed. Only a limited, small number of people stand apart from that and view it all round them with horror. But no one listens to the alarmists and worriers. It is an illusion to think that humanity is going downhill. Only to some people on the periphery—the poets and thinkers, who are always alone—it seems that the human race is changing away from them, whereas it has always been like this. The human race constantly changes fashions and adopts new technologies. But inside, people have never changed. The coarse, gruff, rude, insensitive gorilla who applauds each new gimmick as it makes obsolete the last one is the average human.

Now I'm working on a new biography about Jony Ive [industrial designer at Apple Corp.]. He is a boring, professional, rich, company executive. He turns out products. The CEOs and senior managers all round him calculate the profits and investments. When you read about Apple and the movements of its workers, you read the words "products" "supply chain" "Asian factory" "financial quarter" and so on *ad infinitum*. It is a torture. I couldn't fucking care less about these idiots! Now I'm writing a chapter about Tim Cook, CEO of Apple. This man is fifty-something, never married, graduated in business, and worked in one corporation or other all his career. He is described as a workaholic who often wakes up his subordinate managers with calls and e-mails in the middle of the night, or drags them into conference meetings on Sundays. This behavior is supposed to be admirable. He is a fitness fanatic who goes to the gym every day and relaxes by hiking and cycling. What a boring man. He is worth hundreds of millions of dollars. What is that money doing for him? Just sitting in the bank. Of course he has a huge home and big new cars. But all he does is work. How can any man preoccupy all his hours with thinking about working for his company? And what does his company do, exactly? It churns out products which keep people indoors playing children's games and exchanging texts with their friends. It has reduced the music experience to surfing the net for downloads, then putting thousands of songs on an iPod and never listening to them, or certainly never listening to them in the context of how the musicians presented them—in a music sequence chosen to tell a musical tale (if they are artists). And listen to the sound quality of mp3— has everyone forgotten the fidelity of vinyl records, or live music performed intimately? I could sit in a cornfield and read a brilliant book all day but why am I not allowed to do that?

November 2015

125

A tree doesn't become old but rejuvenates every year. Thus a tree lives forever.

126

To: BAC Home [website forum for left-behind parents in Japan]

Sorry folks, but as long as people want to be removed from mailing lists, no one will face the truth. My two daughters were taken away from me overnight—I went from loving dad to missing person and was ostracized the last six years of their lives. My "wife" (incidentally, foreigners are not actually the spouses of Japanese people, whatever you might think—you are their household "guest") was able and indeed encouraged and assisted in accomplishing my children's total excommunication from their dad and wider non-Japanese family and the way she did that was by enlisting the cooperation of the family court, the kids' school, all neighbors and, most importantly, the police, who warned me not to try to get near my kids. I even lost my job, I strongly suspect, due to my wife's influence. We have all heard similar stories and how can anyone still believe that Japanese people are "totally normal and just like us at heart"? I began as a liberal-minded, cultured, etc., educated product of twenty-first century Britain and then went through a few years of having my hopes and beliefs systematically dismantled. So now I spread the word about what happened to me and so many others from the basis that Japanese people are *not* like anyone else, and that anyone who loses his or her children to Japan will never see them again until a new negotiation strategy is rebuilt starting with "This is what Japanese people *are* like."

I don't often write on this topic nowadays but here I am writing for the third time in a day. First, sorry to all those I offended earlier by saying Japanese people are not normal. I'm sure we all know that that is not true. What I wrote subsequently is further to the point. Colin—if you are still there—I am aware of and admire your work. There are two ways to change opinions in Japan. Yours, which is probably the sole way of achieving success, is long-term studying and teaching in Japan. Mine, which will only work if the idea catches on, is to face the chasm of difference between Japanese and un-Japanese values and say "I don't care what are your values I just want my kids back while they are still kids and I can know them"—which was what I had before they were stolen from me.

This is my last entry as well. As long as people refuse to see that the underlying reason for the epidemic of child abduction in Japan is societal clash of values and that those few of us who acknowledge that are not using "hateful rhetoric" or "racism," but reporting our observations confirmed over and over again, the people who abduct will continue to get away with doing so, with ease, forevermore.

December 2015

127

I'm up in Oxford now. Sitting in a pub reading a book, alone as usual. Next to me a bunch of students whose mostly inane, progressively louder, braying table conversation just produced one good epigram: one of the girls proclaimed "For my dissertation, I write it drunk and edit it sober!" It's freezing cold here (and was raining earlier) but out and about in Oxford tonight we have the widespread spectacle of boys and girls wandering the streets wearing a T-shirt. What a laugh being young is. So is all of life.

128

To Mother—I've spent the last three days with racing fever, delirium, having to run to the toilet every twenty minutes to micturate like fire, awake all night two nights in a row with recurrent hallucinations, went out to get some milk and threw up in the street. Probably bladder infection. I couldn't even go to the doctor, so just sweated it out, literally. Wearing several layers and under two blankets with the fan heater on full, I was shivering with cold. Thus is sickness when you have no one to help look after you. Finally feeling better now.

129

Musicians must tour because their message is fundamentally wrong. No one wants to hear the same musicians all the time. Minstrels, rather than their audience, have to stay on the move.

130

My definition of love: Receiving positive attention.

131

Just watching the football [soccer] on TV. Every player on the pitch has the same brutally shorn military haircut, as do all men in this country. Everyone in Britain has the same army recruit chop, even called a crew cut. Look around. Why is that? Possibly because the current epoch has no music, no daring performers. The Boring 2010s.

London, May 2016

132

Here's my secret of eternal youth: As you get older, do not dismiss anything you dislike about yourself and your circumstances as due to old age.

133

The kind of crap that fills mass-man's minds [newspaper headline "Zika Heading to the Med"]? I couldn't even understand the message (which is why it caught my attention). I thought med referred to medicine (not the Mediterranean) and Zika was some celeb. This headline is an almost exact repeat of one I brought to your attention a few years ago, of how at the start of the holiday season the Ministry of Propaganda always disseminates (via news) a "don't take a holiday, just stay at work in your little badly paid job"-type scare story, each year around beginning of summer holiday period. I've never heard of Zika—I don't pay any attention to news reports.

134

Why did the PowerPoint presentation cross the road? To get to the other slide.
Why did the bigamist cross the road? To get to the other bride.
Why did the road cross the chicken? Because it was an interstate highway thru Kentucky.

I made up those while cycling home earlier. After the first, I had no inclination to remember it. After the second, which spontaneously followed, I also found it a little bit amusing but forgettable. After the third, which jumped into my head again straight away, I thought as a trilogy these are worth documenting!

July 2016

135

Only a woman could say this! I just walked past one on her mobile phone and heard "So what's happening at Silverstone? Eh? Oh, the Grand Prix!"

I'll bet anything her husband / boyfriend has already told her loads of times!

136

Here in the office [temporary contract at Hive Health, a London advertising agency] they're having the "Fun Friday" pursuit which this week is that game where you have something written on your forehead and your opponent (partner) gives you clues to guess it. In this case they're using an iPhone app for it. I wandered over to watch. When the two people who were playing finished, I remarked "So is it a different theme for each player?" while everyone ignored me and talked among themselves. Then because the fellow writer who sits next to me had wandered over as well, the organizer asked her if she wanted to play and pick a partner, so instead of asking me, she scouted off to find someone! The cycle of hatred of me has begun again!

I'm sure my "intellect" (which is from reading literature) causes a lot of hatred and even though I myself feel shy, I've heard plenty of times that I come across as arrogant.

Fuck 'em!!

Just this moment, another colleague walked over so I said, have you played the Friday fun game yet? He replied no what is it? I started to say "It's that game where you put a piece of paper on your…" when someone else ambled over, interrupted over what I was saying, and the two walked off together! Everyone hates me!

Another thing I might do rather a lot is say something "witty" which the person talking hadn't thought of and, even worse, be right about everything! (And more knowledgeable.)

One of the most dreadful things about being hated in an office is the few people who you think *don't* hate you are, rather, indifferent to you so you can't go to them for some sympathy. You just end up with no one to talk to.

A.R.: I reckon the younger ones are okay with you cos to them you are a bit of a curio. The older ones will see you as weird and think you should grow up. Most of them will have given up on life and will resent your whole look and manner. However, the young lot won't like you forever. At some point you'll bore them. People don't like anyone who's a bit different. You'll continue to experience this wherever you work unless you conform.

… and then you'll bore them by conforming….

Useful info about the resentfulness of the "elders." I lost my worldly life six years ago and as a result I appear to be someone who never grew up. I wonder what people would think if they saw me watching *When Marnie Was There*, the Japanese *anime* (cert U), in a cinema on my own last night, crying.

I don't think the youngsters view me as a curio. In my experience of the last three years my own expectation that young people would view me as a natural outsider from their world was disproved over and over again, consistently. As long as you are yourself, and as long as you are not a boring old, joyless, worrier (and conformer!), you can be accepted by young people. But you have to have similar demographics—unmarried, childless, energy and enthusiasm to do similar things, which of course, the vast majority of oldies don't.

137

"You're as young as the woman you feel"—that makes me zero years old!

138

In photography there is an interchangeable 50mm lens known, because of its versatility as somewhere between a pancake lens, a macro, and a zoom, as a "nifty fifty."

Leave that there for now—I'll come back to it.

I cycle to work and there are on my daily journey a whole bunch of cyclists I would estimate are older than I am but because they are going to work, below retirement age. Therefore they are in their fifties. They all wear the same cycle outfit—black tights, yellow jacket, and crash hat. They constantly shout out at cars and pedestrians to "watch where you're going." None of them looks happy in their life. They seem to be strongly smitten by what is known as "entitlement privilege"— an affectation that they are more important than others—reinforced by their age (senior at work but not yet retired, when their price tag will plummet). The managers at my current work are very similar, self-serving, serious grownups. They view me with suspicion, I can tell. Why am I a word-scribbler and not a manager? The answer is I don't want to be a manager. I don't want to hire and fire people and tell them off and interrogate them over their "personal development."

I think these fifty-somethings are a bunch of plebs and they are the reason that no one wants to get old, youngsters don't like them and dread becoming one.

Not long from now, I'll be fifty and will have resisted turning into a pleb for five decades. I'm gonna be a "nifty fifty."

139

Sitting in my local Japanese restaurant. Next table dominated by a motor-mouth large woman who hasn't shut up once. Her tiresome conversation, all about herself and what she "knows," flits from the questionably informed surface of one topic to the next at a rate of about two seconds per subject. From overhearing similar conversations every day, it seems that the population, fed on TV, newspapers, and the internet, has lost its ability to concentrate, or understand in depth, anything.

I lost my job again yesterday and my manager who fired me talks like the person here. Creativity at that ads agency was conjured together by a notion that medical decision making is done on the basis of a rudimentary, superficial feeling for what might work best, especially if suggested by a visiting sales rep brandishing a cartoon comic strip. Perhaps it is.

140

… and an unbelievable level of self-importance out of all proportion with sanity. This is a society where people who are borderline illiterate and can hardly write an e-mail without basic spelling errors use their aggressiveness to hold onto a job. When these people become managers their self-preservation is unstoppable. They're overdosed on TV and newspapers. Look at the back pages of all newspapers. You will see faces of very rich sports persons contorted in a warrior frenzy. These people are lionized as the winners of society. Aggressiveness and winning are the highest prizes.

One of the most oft-used statements made by competitive office managers whose egos have driven them power mad is "Anyone can lose their job nowadays—I can even lose mine!" However, their job is never under any threat; they rose to where they are mainly by luck and keep their job as long as they please.

141

Here's how I'd describe the last company I contracted [Hive Health]. They're in medical advertising. No one there knows anything about the pharmaceutical industry. They dropped me when they realized the gulf between my knowledge and theirs is not helpful to them. Anyway, a couple weeks ago, the HR woman sent me a letter in the post asking me to return the entrance security pass, which I had forgotten to hand in on my last day. It's a plastic card no different to the kind of room key hotels lose by the handful every day. I thought I'd drop it off next time I'm in town—I go to central London often enough.

Last Friday, I remembered that I'm owed money for a few days I worked in September before I left that ads agency. They hadn't paid me, so I phoned in. The first thing the (same as above) HR woman lied was they hadn't paid because my invoice was late. I said no it wasn't, I sent it to you on my last day a month ago. It was a month early. Ignoring that, she asked me about my security pass. I said I would drop it off personally in the next few days. She said why don't I mail it if that's more convenient. I said it's not more convenient it's less convenient. Every time I go to a post office there's a long line. You don't need it in a hurry and I'll drop it off soon, I added. Then I said anyway I didn't call about the security pass I want to know when I'm going to receive my pay for September. Her answer: "When we receive the security pass." Talentless, thick, gang of racketeers who protect themselves inside a guarded barracks and mistreat employees past and present with arbitrary, unaccountable actions. And individuals can do nothing because the companies have the law on their side every time.

The so-called "Intelligentsia" are the least intelligent people. In society, the strongest are the rich, then the masses, and the "Intelligentsia" last.

October 2016

142

A.R.: I'm fascinated [by some claims that Paul McCartney died and was replaced in The Beatles by a lookalike "Billy" in 1966—inspired by an altered resemblance]. What makes it so interesting is we will never know the truth.

Let's try an experiment—look at pics of footballers [soccer players]. Even today, they all have their "cigarette card" portrait taken every season. It would be easy to find pics of young footballers professionally photographed aged twenty, five years ago, and again aged twenty-five today. If the facial differences do not exceed those in the Macca conspiracy [pics of McCartney taken before and after the so-called switch], then it's just that, a hoax.

My main objection is Jane Asher. Let's say "Billy" was drafted into the Fabs with a promise of millions and he roped in his parents / associates to keep the secret on the grounds that they would all prosper. That secret, offered Macca's fortune, could be kept. But would Jane Asher simply become Billy's lover at the time? (She dated Macca before and after 1966.) If she married "Billy," then maybe, but she didn't—Linda did. Upon the split, she would have told everyone—unless she were replaced as well!

I just did the experiment I suggested over pics of a footballer. Searching for "footballer born in 1991" I found Oscar. He played in South America as a youth and moved to Chelsea in 2012, aged twenty-one. Perfect. Then I searched images—there are plenty of those. In a Chelsea strip he is playing aged over twenty-one; in another club strip he is under twenty-one. Scrolling through lots of pics, including obvious childhood and teenage pics, his face is always undeniably recognizable. This suggests (and I only checked this one person) that faces don't change very much over youth. So: either "Billy" is really an imposter or the suggestion that Macca was replaced by a lookalike influences our eyes to see differences. Who knows!

143

I'm always astonished by all the many ingenious new ways to rip you off that people in Britain devise. Here are a few that happened to me recently.

Scam 1

I got a speeding ticket which arrived in the post with the usual devious wording used by scammers (in this case the police). "The penalty for exceeding the speed limit is up to £1,000. However, to avoid prosecution you can pay £100 by [insert date]." The letter was dated something like end of April but arrived mid-May. This gave me only fourteen days, not the stated twenty-eight days, to comply. I paid the £100 by phone but couldn't find my license so I called the cops. They said if the license were not surrendered by the deadline my £100 would be reimbursed and the case go to court. Needless to say, when this inevitably happened I received a letter from the magistrates demanding to know my means. I wrote back I'm broke, £20,000 in debt, and have been unemployed for most of the last twelve months. I also added that it was not my fault that I did not have sufficient time to surrender my license, and that this minor speeding offence was my first traffic violation in twenty-five years on the road. The outcome: fine increased six times over to £635. This notification bore the phone number to pay the enhanced fine, in bold, three times on both sides of the paper. At the bottom was "What to do if you have difficulty paying": contact the Traffic Enforcement Agency. No phone number was given for this. So I looked it up—an office in Northampton. I called and went through diverse voice recordings before getting through to a human. Finally I was told: "We do not issue the penalties, we only collate them here. Contact your local authority." I just gave up and called the number to pay, begged a bit, and managed to have the fine broken down into six monthly instalments of £100 each. This was confirmed with a nasty letter a few days later listing all the adverse outcomes that could happen to me if I tried any nonsense. That was long so more scams later!

Scam 2

Recently I went for an interview to work as an employee at a med comms agency [Chameleon, in Ealing] and was thrilled to receive an offer of being hired as a freelancer initially, with an option to "come onboard" permanently at the end of the year—a full three months ahead. It was music to my ears—I could keep trading as my own company, when I had nearly given up hope. I started and did some typical work. At the end of the third day, I reported to my manager that I had done what I was asked and she replied "Well I don't have anything else to give you now, why don't you speak to the director." So I went to the director and she said "I'll ask around the teams and see what more there is for you to do. We'll call you." It was 5:30 p.m. so I went home. When I got in, I received a text and an e-mail saying "We are not satisfied with your work quality. You do not need to come back." I thought eh? 1) no one has had time to review the work, which I delivered only about an hour before 2) the work is my usual, high standard 3) I would always expect to review work with my manager 4) if it were not as expected normally, between us, we would decide how to rectify it. I was only there three days. In any case, my contract stipulated that either party had to give the other two weeks' leave of notice—the first thing I checked when I signed the contract. The next day, I went to Citizens Advice. They read the contract and pointed out that underneath the clause about two weeks' notice was a subclause: "During the two-week notice period, the company will only pay the contractor for work that is agreed in writing in advance." I said in what way is that giving me two weeks' notice? "It doesn't," she replied, "You've been scammed!"

Scam 3

This morning I received a letter from Smart (Mercedes Benz) saying my motor insurance policy is due for renewal and included the new documents to return.

When I bought the car a year ago, its most attractive features were the no road tax (low emissions) and Mercedes's own insurance, £115 per year. The new insurance letter said "Please note, we no longer offer Mercedes insurance." The new policy: £550. Yes, a nearly £450 increase. (I thought insurance was supposed to go down each year?) I phoned and, unlike when I phoned to book in my one-year service (price £200), where I got through to a well-mannered rep straight away, this time was shunted around several answering machines and different reps who "put me on hold while we transfer you to the right department"—with long waits listening to awful music—and finally got through to a council estate chav who explained that "Last year's offer was a promotion that is no longer available." I said do you really expect your customers to be happy to have their insurance premiums hiked up five times higher after one year? These ill-educated telephone reps expect you to accept from them terms which they themselves would never tolerate if the other way round. How they can keep a straight face is beyond me. "That offer was a promotional offer which is no longer available to customers." Nice scam eh?

144

A masterpiece of pretentious drivel [by Matthew Syed, *The Times* Sports Journalist of the Year].

145

Pushing fifty is not really a big deal for me. I try not to think about my age as a number. It's like I never watch TV. There are many things in life that are tailored to put you down, which I have described repeatedly over the years. Unwittingly, you are fooled by TV. Even reading this will anger you (because TV has won). There is nothing wrong with being fifty in itself. There are only personal flaws, which anyone can choose to fix.

I have not once brought it up (turning fifty), only you have. It seems that you are worried about it. I have only denied that I'm fifty (I'm not yet, and certainly wasn't when you started telling me I am some years ago). But mostly, I deny what you really mean, is the implications of "being fifty"—old, past it, unsexy, irrelevant, tired out, grumpy, unhappy, bitter, cynical, all things that I know I am not. I deny being a supposed typical fifty year old, as depicted on TV and in the news. Here are some things you've written to me recently: I have to get an office haircut. I have to wear normal clothes as worn by fifty-year-olds on TV. No young woman could be possibly interested in a fifty year old. All these go against my observations, so I disbelieve them. They are foisted on the public by TV and newspapers, in such subtle ways that no one cares to notice.

The young versus old thing is a constant theme in the news. The other day a female schoolteacher aged around thirty was in the news having fucked two seventeen-year-old boys in her classes. The news claimed the shame of it and how the twisted pervert had manipulated those innocent boys. I disagree. All persons involved were tempted into it and the temptation is a natural instinct. No one got hurt, leave them to it. Same with the footballer recently who, aged twenty-something, had a "sex act" (undisclosed, but not intercourse it seems) with a fifteen-year-old girl. Now he's in prison. These young-old anti-sex attitudes are constantly reinforced in the news. The story about the debauched female teacher was followed, I remember, in the same newspaper by a "Britain Swelters in Heatwave" story—a selection of pictures of teenage girls in bikinis, chosen for their attractiveness, on the beach.

This is what TV does: all couples are identically aged. When a single man seeks a partner, it is scripted that he goes for a similarly aged woman. Remember [U.K. TV show] *Blind Date*? The age range of contestants was very limited to say twenty to twenty-five. Then there was an oldies version (over sixty-fives, limited to around age seventy for decency), and maybe a forties version? I don't remember exactly. I watched a movie on Netflix the other day: some grownup man was looking after an autistic kid in a road movie. Selena Gomez (aged twenty maybe) played the obligatory pretty hitchhiker *en route*. When they offered her a ride, she asked the forty-something "You're not a pervert are you?" A pervert! I would say that a man who is *not* interested in pretty young women is a pervert—or at least, repressed. Every straight man who watches that film would like to fuck Selena Gomez and so the movie's message to its audience is "You are a pervert." I disagree. Why does TV reinforce these notions? Because the role of TV is to present a vision of normality for everyone to swallow. Who wants everyone to be normal? Our controllers of course. The last thing they want is a revolution.

A.R.: Are you not middle-aged then?

No, in that I don't conform to what that means to people—that's my objection. It carries with it the nuance "old and boring" which I'm not. I'm not penny pinching, mistrustful, weary, cautious, jaded, any of those connotations, so I resent the title. And I haven't declined physically since I was thirty—I still run round the youngsters at football. The expectation to become worn out and boring is just a myth—as you discovered in your own case, and mine. Most people become old because the news tells them to think that. I'm not what I'm expected to be.

December 2016

146

To: The British Embassy Japan, Tokyo

Hello, this is a message regarding my two children, Selene and Cale, who were abducted by their Japanese mother in Japan, April 2010. At the time, I was living in Japan and reported the abduction to the British Embassy in Tokyo—you should have a record of these events. By abduction, I mean that my wife moved out with the children to another apartment and refused to allow me to see or speak to my children again. Their lives were then spent either in school or kept inside their apartment. If I ever tried to get close to my children, my wife or the children's school would call the police who could arrest me. Having subsequently lost my job, I was unable to continue living in Japan and moved to U.K. in 2013.

I write because a few months ago, I asked a friend who was visiting Japan to check on the apartment where I last knew my wife and children were living. It seems currently empty. So I would like to know where my children are now—please could the embassy help out.

[No response from British Embassy]

147

This week's attractive young person killed. Let's have a Christmas filled with bad cheer and worry, courtesy of our newspapers and TV, everybody!

148

Just bought Stephen Dobyns's latest book of poetry [*Copper Beech*]. It's his first new book since [2010's] *Winter's Journey*, which I remember reading in the *onsen* [hot springs] at Yamanakako. If I were reading a book in the bath, it means I went alone. It must have been after the abduction. Looking down the list of Dobyns' book titles, I bought the last five as soon as they were published—going back to 1999. The one before that, published 1996, was already in the shops before I knew about Stephen Dobyns (who started publishing poetry in the early 1970s). I remember the first time I discovered Dobyns—I was in a bookshop in Hampstead, browsing the poetry section, and gave Dobyns a try. I was captivated, and have loved his poetry ever since. That must have been late '90s, and I was in my twenties. Then, I fervently believed that I would become a successful writer and that one day my books would be in all bookstores.

149

Opening a book at random… is not at all random, and is instead nearly always within a few pages of the halfway mark.

London, January 2017

150

Life P.O.N.G.S. (Post No One Gives a Shit). Can't say I'm truly there yet.

151

Here's a mystery for you. It has happened a few times before, most recently when I returned back from San Francisco last week. I got the feeling that someone has been in my flat while I was away. Not a feeling, signs. Such as, some shoes kicked over—something that I myself would pick up. Not long ago it was a towel folded differently to how I do it. These are things that an intruder—if indeed there were one—may not know are giving him away. Now my hypothesis. There have been a lot of people, all youngsters, in and out my house during the last couple years since I started playing in Richmond music scene. One of those people is a self-made homeless man of upper class origins with whom I fell out a while ago. I suspect he helped himself to a spare key from my kitchen drawer and uses my flat as a warm dry space when he knows I'm away, such as at Christmas. I will ask my landlord to change the locks but mostly I'm intrigued—I enjoy a mystery to solve, and changing the locks won't inform the person "I know who you are."

152

Why was Jupiter, a planet who is occasionally visible, the king of the Gods whereas the Sun was Apollo, a lesser God? Also Helen (Moon)?

153

For some reason, this morning I thought "I've not talked to anyone all week, all I've done is hang around in Kew or traveled to central London and wandered about on my own. I need to do something different." So I drove to Shropshire and have been looking at my childhood home, school, my Granddad's house, old friends' houses, and so on. Shifnal is just a village amid countryside and was practically deserted this afternoon. I went to my old school and there was a football [soccer] match on. They were playing on the same pitch I used to play. I thought "Blimey these guys are good. Like pros." Then I noted that the school is nowadays a sports college. I headed back towards the high street through an old council estate [public housing] when I passed one of the few pedestrians out and about I had seen all day. A dog walker, young bloke. As he walked past me, I was shocked—he had the raw, harsh face, clothes, and overall appearance of something from the 1970s. I thought perhaps nothing changes out here in the middle of nowhere. He was listening to music on some kind of pocket device—it was playing thrash punk, not loud.

I then went to look at my primary school, and cut back through the village churchyard. I started to remember something, that a friend's big brother's friend got killed by a car and was buried there. I tried to remember the name—he was friends with Nick Collins' brother. A name came back to me Kirk—Fielding. I tried to remember the face and got an impression. He was one of the village's tiny population of punks. In a punk band. Among a row of not-so-old graves, there it was—not Kirk Fielding, Shaun Fisher, older brother of Carl Fisher. He was a teen when I was a boy. He used to rough me up, but playfully. His brother Carl, also older, used to teach me football tricks. They were council kids through and through. During everything I have done in my life over the last nearly forty years, Shaun has been in that grave. Then I remembered the dog walker from earlier—Shaun's absolute image. His ghost, no doubt at all. Maybe not literally his spirit walking around the council estate where he lived his short life, but a necessary encounter for today's travels. I wonder whether apart from his family (there were flowers on the grave), anyone else has remembered him in years. I am convinced he appeared today. Playing punk music. The dog walker was something trapped in the past.

154

Today's memorial ramble included this disused power station at Coalbrookdale. These towers are gargantuan. Immense. Way bigger than Battersea. Anyway, the reason that I came to look today was because when I was thirteen, fourteen, my best mate (Dave Onions)'s folks would go to a pub somewhere around here and bring us along. Dave and I would play football. They also bought Dave and me half a lager. I sipped it once and thought that is disgusting. It was my first taste of beer (not alcohol *per se*) and I probably spat it out. My main priority was taking a free kick, not beer.

155

Currently re-reading a brilliant tome [*Asimov's Guide to Science*], which I first read when I was a teen. It certainly helped foster my interest in physics when I was at school. Anyway, I was thinking about the scientific view of the creation of the universe, some thousand millions of years ago. According to science, the inchoate universe was a super-dense conglomeration of matter that suddenly exploded during the Big Bang and sent the galaxies rocketing through space in what can now be seen as the expanding universe. Prior to this event, there was no time and no physical matter.

In what way is this less silly than God created the universe? The only difference between the hypotheses is that the Big Bang was an instantaneous unprecedented event, whereas God took seven days. If anything, seven days seems more likely, for an entire universe!

156

I just received a letter in the post from my landlord. As I nervously opened it, it turned out to be a contract for my next year's lease, *at no rent increase*. This is the first non-hostile communication I have received from a landlord, employer, service provider, in years. As I opened it, I was dreading an eviction notice. My unremitting bad experiences over the last few years have turned me into a paranoid schizophrenic, like someone who has been in a concentration camp.

157

In *Life & Nihonjin* I asked the question "Are our lives a pre-set storyline from which we have no choice but to enact?"—in other words are our free will and sense that things transpire around us according to what others do merely illusions? I know no one who has understood this question, let alone who also has asked it. No one who has read my book has ever mentioned it as its central point, which I set out emphatically, twice. I'm asking, is it all predetermined? An example would be Leicester City F.C. surprising everyone by winning the Premier League last year—but what if all the teammates were born to do that, already decided?

158

My Cale's birthday today. I haven't spoken to my daughters in seven years. Seven years of bad luck—did I break a mirror?

159

I don't follow the news so don't know anything about Donald Trump. Don't forget my decision to boycott TV was because of the nervous damage I realized was done to me by his predecessors' entourage, starting with Bush, Fox News, CNN, etc., in early 2000s. I have not watched TV or read a newspaper since shortly after 9/11, when as I wrote to you at the time, I realized the news media are more sinister than mere manipulators trying to convince you to believe their agenda in a way that you can give or take, but better than that: their message will get to you as long as you receive it because they are experts committed to deceiving you for their own ends and will always hide that. They're professional. It's not only news that I avoid—it's TV full stop. Dramas are even worse for you than the news, more subtle in the ways they insidiously shape your ideas about the world. Even comedy, supposedly looking ironically, actually reaffirms your illusions. And the news even pretends to criticize its rich paymasters, a lot. I'd rather read a good book!

February 2017

160

I just listened to "Penny Lane" over and over again. Weeping profusely. Think my whole life is in that song.

161

One day last summer my mate Laurence span a 10p coin on my kitchen counter which slowed and slowed and eventually stopped upright on its edge, about three centimeters from the wall. For some reason we both intently watched over that happening, despite there being other people in the kitchen who had not witnessed it, and we both laughed when it stayed upright. He then spun another coin on the counter, and this one started to wander. It slowly arced round (precessed), gradually approached the still-standing previous coin, and improbably passed between it and the wall, without touching either. Again, our heads were hovered above this event watching intently.

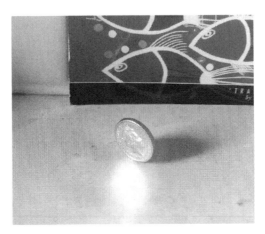

162

Watched Woody Allen's superb *Match Point* last night. I noted (to myself) recently that "Woody Allen is the Man of the Century"—twentieth and twenty-first. Like Shakespeare he span the end of one century and the beginning of the next. I think Allen is the Shakespeare of this age. *Match Point* is his *Macbeth*. It's a spot-on study of what people are like—so actually not *Macbeth*—more *Timon of Athens*—and focuses on something I have written about a lot—how luck, not ability, guides our lives.

163

Yes been doing that [controlling expenditure] for the last eighteen months. In case you haven't noticed, I've been out of work for the majority of that time. You can't piss money if you don't have any. You piss nothing.

164

The central deception of the mass media is squarely encapsulated in the lie: "The news cannot criticize the Royal Family because they are prevented from speaking out, and therefore from defending themselves, in public." This one lie alone ought to provoke a bloody revolution. It means: "You don't say anything bad about the establishment, because we own you." The news constantly censures whomever it pleases who "can't answer back." The news ruins people's reputations every day. Indeed, the news is the only means there is for anyone to answer back—and the Royals put out their sanitized message via their press office all the time. Unlike, for example, the deceased Jimmy Saville [posthumously despised U.K. TV personality]. I still don't know what Saville is supposed to have done. And yet he is the most reviled (dead) man in Britain. The entire purpose of mass media (TV, newspapers) is to broadcast a stereotypical portrayal of normality for its stupefied audience to absorb. Every day. All day. And it works beautifully for the TV program controllers (program controllers—what does that imply?). Back to the above. Long ago, at the start of the mass media, the establishment who agreed to allowing its inception—in its own terms, naturally (instead of banning it)—would have formulated the above agreement as a nod-and-a-wink handshake that still remains in place. Thus the Royals can get on with exploiting us inferiors with impunity, and commit their crimes such as the (to my mind) obvious undercover murder of Princess Di, whom I once spotted at an open-air Pavarotti concert, and whose funeral cortege I witnessed not long after.

The Tudor heirs of Henry VIII—Edward VI, Mary I, Elizabeth I, all had their mothers murdered. What a family.

Governing is infinitely complex, but the overall result is those at the top protect their position.

165

Remember when I correctly pointed out that the system of grouping people by their teens, twenties, thirties, etc. is misleading and a much better grouping would be the mid-points birth to five, six to fifteen, sixteen to twenty-five, twenty-six to thirty-five....

April 2017

166

Only when I catch him [Bruce Welch] doing nothing. I see him most mornings [in local café] but he's usually talking to someone. This morning, I said Hey Bruce I got a question… he span round and dropped his cup of tea, so that was a good start. "So Bruce, did Macca die and get replaced?" Laughter: "No! I know him, so no." And there you go, straight from the horse's mouth.

167

I didn't elaborate on what I think about football [soccer] and big sports events in general. Like pubs, they are rowdy gatherings—yet permitted. Why? Remember raves in the '90s. They were known as "love-ins"—very popular secretive all-nighters exclusively for the young whose drugs were the chemical ecstasy and the physical drug, sex. The music was psychedelic trance. Those were large, well organized events. The authorities actively sought them out and clamped them down. Why? Because they had no control over them. But they do control major sports. Every football match is a large police operation. So football is allowed by the authorities, why? I think it's because football encapsulates all the same attributes that the authorities stuff down the people's throats as they do with TV and newspapers. Football is about teams and hard work and winners. Every team has a manager who is old and young players. Footballers themselves are wholesome with regulation haircuts and talk about "doing it for the team, not myself"—yet they jump ship at every opportunity for more money. They don't drink—they have to keep fit. They also marry and have children while young—the only section of society that does that in their early twenties. They are clearly encouraged to do so. If you don't fit in, you don't get picked to play. I don't think matches are fixed—there is no need to do that because fan loyalty transcends their team's fortunes. Some of the biggest and most ardently supported teams have been in lower divisions for years—Aston Villa (European Cup winners in '80s), Newcastle, Leeds. The only time I thought "That was a fix" was the 1998 World Cup final in France, when Brazil's Ronaldo, then the best player on the planet, had an "epileptic seizure" just before the game and couldn't play. Brazil were rubbish despite dominating the tournament till then and home team France won. I think on that occasion, with all the millions spent by the host nation to stage the World Cup, only victory would justify the cost. At any cost.

168

You know I don't read the newspapers but you can't escape headlines because they're thrust in your face. The controllers who devise them make sure of that. So I'm aware that the latest scare is "Russia and U.S. on Brink of Nuclear War!" Hmm. Heard that one before. It was rammed down my neck throughout my childhood.

Let's say the Russkies and Uncle Sam had an all-out nuclear war. We'd all die, right? Wrong. There would be survivors. And those survivors would inherit the Earth. Who would be those lucky survivors? People, everywhere. How come? Take the case of Hiroshima. It flattened Hiroshima alright. But nowhere else. Many people survived in Hiroshima, and the bomb killed no one farther out. If one landed on Birmingham, for instance, we in London wouldn't even hear it. But what about the deadly radiation? That's bullshit as well. I worked on a long-term study in Japan, which concluded that the incidence rate of cancers was no higher in Hiroshima / Nagasaki than elsewhere in Japan and other countries over the ensuing sixty years. Both cities were immediately rebuilt and re-inhabited straight after the war and today are big, busy, modern cities. So much for the Earth will be uninhabitable. If there were an all-out nuclear war, the real losers would be the controllers, top military men, and industrialists who are the only people involved in declaring wars anyway, and so would never allow themselves to lose, for once. So why do the newspapers proclaim war is in the air? Yawn. To keep the people scared, of course. Even those who "know it's all bullshit." There's only one way to immunize yourself from the powers of control—refuse to see it. It is in every word of the newspapers and every broadcast on TV, every single one.

One more skulking villain in your all-out mind control is another institution I refuse to patronize—supermarkets.

169

According to the *Daily Mirror* we're on the brink of nuclear war but the *Sun* considers an insult to a big-titted celeb is more important news.

170

What about when work gives you your marching orders and you do the Walk o' Shame never to be seen again—but, however, your name lives on as the subject of slander ever after, such as "Oh him—he was useless" "I had to let him go" etc. Thus is your unfair dismissal justified!

Q: What do you call an Irishman who gets the boot at work?
A: Seamus Walker!

May 2017

171

Last night I had several choices—hang out with some friends on Richmond Green, see a band I know, or attend a birthday party. Instead, I went to my local pub and watched a masterclass from Messi in El Clásico. You can be lonely amid people who love you.

172

Just read a very brilliant book in a single three-hour sitting—*Ways of Seeing* by John Berger. Last sentence encapsulates why I have refused to watch TV or read a newspaper for the last fifteen or so years (actually lost interest in TV even longer ago).

I have said over and over that the role of TV is to keep you down—to show you a set of modest aspirations to aim at over your life that, even if you were to achieve them all, would still place you as a poor nobody.

173

I have nightmares all the time so usually don't wake up during one and think "That was disturbing." I think "That was a normal dream for me." Here was this morning's (saved by my alarm clock). I entered a horror house, in daylight, followed by sinister children, say older children not quite teens. At first I thought the hallway wall was spattered in blood—but it was a large poster of a world map. I knew I was in a movie. In the next chamber was a chef, who was violently chopping. He turned round and had the deranged face of a man starting old age. On the table were parts of a chopped-up child—arms and chunks—in *tempura* batter. I fled the house. In the slow motion of trying to get away in dreams. The children followed me. The next several scenes were my attempts to run away—shinning up and crawling along the branches of trees and by clambering over walls—all precariously and with my pursuers right behind. Finally I was on an open road and a tram [trolley car] started moving towards me. I crossed the road and continued my attempt to flee along the top of a low wall next to a churchyard, as someone ran up behind me. Then my alarm awoke me.

This dream was, like most my dreams (nightmares), yet another yarn of my youth coming back to bother me. The chef was a demented old man devouring a child, and childhood followed me around, threateningly. The connection with food (the chopped-up child in *tempura* batter) might be because I was talking to myself as I headed out for dinner last night, that when you lose the ability to attract female company, you find something else to give you pleasure, like food. But the strange thing about the dream, and this is how clever and informative dreams are and why they are always worth trying to decode—all my spellbound means of escape from childhood were exactly what in my wake state I think of as connections to my childhood: I often climb trees and I always walk along atop a wall if I see one on my way.

174

The way to stay young is to retain the schoolboy sense of humor—and this in turn can only be done if one retains the schoolboy outlook itself. This outlook is a simple black-'n'-white ethic of right 'n' wrong encoded as the "Law of the Playground." Indeed, it is the gradual erosion of the Law of the Playground in the hearts of the people that causes them to become old: each time they break the law of right 'n' wrong out of self-interest they must concoct some casuistry that they did not make any transgression—and it is the steady build-up of self-deceptions that eventually replaces beyond recognition the schoolboy: the grownup becomes a shadow of falsity.

175

One of the most egregious and sickening phenomena on TV is the creation of "loveable" working-class stereotypes (I don't watch TV but these may have been latterly replaced by "celebrity" chavs of the worst kind). Back in the day, the *Sun* newspaper, the rag that controls the rabble, would feature stories about [popular U.K. TV characters] "Del Boy" and "Dirty Den" as though they really existed. Now they focus on the equally unreal lives of the talentless morons they make famous. No wonder people can't tell the difference between TV and real life experience, which is benign and kind if you want it to be.

176

A.R.: You do realise (don't you?) that talking about "not reading papers" "not watching TV" etc. is turning you into what people will refer to as "that weird bloke"? You are actually brainwashing yourself, to avoid what you think is brainwashing out there in the media. To opt out of everything means that in a very short space of time you'll have no valid or informed opinion on anything.

But I opted out many years ago. However, I have not opted out of looking around at my surroundings and reading much more useful stuff, like books. Do you think people had no idea how to live before TV came along? And I have no valid opinions?

A.R.: You know what I mean! The media, papers, TV, Twitter, fake news, wiki leaks... it's all shit but you can't ignore it.

I can and do ignore it. I'm not saying you have to. For me it was therapeutic and I never looked back. The observation that TV is a drug is indisputable in that it has the properties of being injurious and people cannot quit—yourself included. I've described why TV is harmful many times. It is one of the tools that keep you down and I would say—although I bet you will deny—that on the few occasions when you and I have argued about something and my opinion is unusual (even though I stick by it) and your counter-argument is what everyone thinks and therefore must be indubitable because common sense—I would say that in those instances your assurance is in each case "proven" by media rather than any rigorous investigation, whereas my controversial opinion was garnered by testing the conventional wisdom and disproving it, to my mind. What everyone believes is common sense might be what everyone has been exposed to by media, rather than their experiences.

177

[The late '70s–early '80s sci-fi comic book *2000AD*] … early taught me not only that things ain't what they seem but also, crucially, that kids could know better and may question adult bullshit. This, from a young age, greatly freed me to think for myself.

178

Shakespeare was elevated to status of Britain's national poet because his most popular plays are the power struggles with which the commoners can identify: *Hamlet, King Lear, Macbeth, Romeo and Juliet*—whereas his greatest plays, the arcana *Tempest / Measure for Measure* and the pessimistic *Timon of Athens*, are the least well known and hardly performed.

179

I can't listen to politicians, prime ministers, newscasters, full stop. Every utterance is a lie.

180

I occasionally experience this little epiphany. I perceive a bloke in what I would estimate is his mid-thirties, who's overweight and looks worn out, and in rapid fire the following associations flash through my mind: he's only about my age—wait I'm not in my thirties—my thirties are over—hang on, what!—my forties are over...!

It's a shock every time. It happens very quickly but in each of those steps. This is what worries me as the boat-keeper prepares to call in Boat No. 50. My total conviction, starting from a young age, that I was going to "make it," (rich or at least have some money) appears to have been unfounded (although there still remain a few years left to carry on giving it a go). I'm scared not because of that alone so much, but rather the absolute conviction I had means I never envisaged a plan B based on the alternative hypothesis that I would not make it rich. I'm looking at a future of poverty.

My elderly neighbor Peter is a constant reminder of what the future might look like to me. Indeed, the Great Powers in the Sky probably put him there on purpose. He lives alone, but still fancies young women ("Phwoar look at that one over there!"), drinks a few glasses of wine every night, and goes on about his next musical extravaganza he's going to produce. I found him on movie databases as a "film impresario"—of nothing. Last weekend Peter asked me about my new car because he's thinking of replacing his corroding antique Volvo. I said I'd take him to the sales showroom and he could check out models (car models, that is). Yesterday when I knocked on his door, he told me that economically he was going to stick with the Volvo. He's broke. My biggest worry is I'm turning into Peter.

181

My view on 9/11 has not changed since soon after the events—a barely credible coverup perpetrated by politician / military types banking on the blind trust / gullibility / indifference of the public. They pulled it off at the time and have all got away with it. Their overall aim was to protect themselves from possible threats and, as throughout history, perpetuate a status quo with themselves at the top of the entire human race, insulated from a vast worldwide population many stages below by a large national population just several steps below.

182

I've been meaning to write this for a while. I have a friend-of-a-friend, who is actually personably very matey to me. At least whenever I meet him we always get on well and have a chuckle. He's a Goth. But, he's at least thirty, I'd say mid-thirties. He's a Goth—long raven hair, thick make-up, black Goth garb. Full-time Goth. I used to think always, "Shouldn't he grow up?" I know him via my young crowd of friends but whereas I make no secret of my age, and indeed do nothing but be myself regardless of with whom I am, I used to muse that the above person was trying to appear younger than he is so as to ingratiate himself with genuinely young people. That perturbed me.

Then I applied La Rochefoucauld's teachings to myself instead of towards others all the time. I considered, if this Goth fella has not crossed me in any way, and is indeed always friendly to me, why does he annoy me? Applying Rochefoucauld, there is only one answer. That I envy him. He has young girlfriends, dresses how he pleases, and is popular. It cemented a valuable lesson—that Rochefoucauld cannot be refuted and that, as Rochefoucauld tells us, our envies and jealousies are blind, as are all our motivations.

183

Great artists often may be so obsessed with one particular theme that it recurs in all their work. Or rather, it is all they want to show. Rochefoucauld is one, Oscar Wilde another. Leonardo painted the same woman's face over and over again— his Goddess. If you ever visit the National Gallery in London, one of the most edifying and spiritual rooms is that containing the obsessive paintings of Claude Lorrain—scene after scene of a ship preparing to depart into the sunset over a pink sea, the harbor a crumbling set of desolate temples and ruined palaces. Another obsessive, fabulous painter is Caspar David Friedrich.

184

There's been an operetta of squeals of *"Oooh sweeeeets!"* among the office ladies this week, with several "fun" happenings and people returning from holidays loaded with chocs etc. It really does seem an essential part of office harmoniousness to evince exaggerated enthusiasm for something you could go out and buy for a few pence. I guess women feel they have to squeal *"Sweets!"* in the same way I was forced to get a short haircut and wear boring work clothes to keep this job.

185

Poe is a cult writer. Everyone has heard of him, probably knows the titles of a few of his stories, certainly is aware he penned "The Raven" or "horror stories"—but the numbers of people who have actually read Poe's tales (of the Grotesque and Arabesque) are few, and those who have read him extensively are a minuscule minority. Poe is a cult writer. Why? His characters are all brilliant seers and perspicacious wits, who *cerebrate*. Or, they are haunted madmen tortured by their own depth of feeling—mourning or regret or betrayal. I started thinking this in response to your question this morning, over why Graham Hancock isn't touched by the mainstream. Same as Poe—the mainstream avoids thinkers. The mainstream is there to stop you from thinking. It presents you its message in the form of a series of "facts," termed "bulletins," "reports," and so on. They never say, hey what do you think of this?—which is my response to all news that comes my way. And what I think is, why do I need to know this? Why are they telling me this? If you read Poe and the likes of Poe you will be better equipped for life than by taking in TV or the news, the diet of un-thinkers.

London, September 2017

186

Today's beautiful young person to die prematurely. There's usually one on the front page news, where you can't miss it, every week. A *memento mori*, these are designed to remind you that you can die at any minute, that you should be scared, and the safest place where you know that no one will do you any harm is your workplace, so run and hide in there because the outside world is scary!

187

Happy Friday from The Establishment! Why is this young man's death front-page news?

188

Autumn began last Saturday. Prior to then, for a few weeks because the temperature dropped certain people were saying "Summer's over, autumn's here," but it wasn't. Autumn began last Saturday. Autumn is not a change of weather, it's a mood.

189

Been pondering. My last (proper) holiday was in 2006. My younger brother got hitched in San Francisco and we went to that. My daughters were nearly five and three, my wife just thirty. That heralded the end of that life. A week later, the night after returning to Tokyo, I came off my motorbike and spent sixteen nights in hospital. That was the end of that life. I have often asked this: Did I die that night and am I now in limbo? My wife started to become the nightmare she would develop into, then. In control of our finances, she lied that we could not afford a holiday every subsequent year after that final excursion. The date of the motorbike crash was 9/11, which has traditionally, since 2001, been an unlucky day for me. This year's 9/11 just passed, without incident. From 2006 to 2017 is eleven years. Eleven years in limbo, and seven years' bad luck, seem fitting and propitious numbers. Now I think, I hope, they are over.

October 2017

190

Just went past Latimer Road [Tube station] on my way to Baker Street where I'm working today. When I last ventured this way, a week after the Grenfell Tower conflagration, the train was packed with ghoulish voyeurs there to see the charred remains of the block. The tower is still there, looking even worse now—more corroded as though it might fall down. Today, however, not one person looked up as we passed the tower. They all just tapped away at their phones, indifferent. The newspapers thrive absolutely on the minuscule memory spans of the people.

191

Men are fragile egos which makes them suckers for swindlers who offer up insubstantial fantasies.

192

You watched the TV movie adaptation, and read, [Stephen King's novella] *1922*, right? Then you will remember that in the book the driving need of the man to retain his farm was resistance to corporate takeover by pig factories. That kept coming up in the novella—that his wife wanted to sell up to the factories and that his neighbor had done so and that every farm in the state had gone the same way. Why did that element of the original story not appear in the movie version? I'll leave you to know why. TV is corrupted and each broadcast is designed, by the program controllers, to keep you in your place. I repeat my message once again: the only way to escape from the influence of TV, just like the only way to escape being a heroin addict, is not to go near it. It's true you have to pick and choose what to include in a movie representation but the main point of *1922* was the protagonist did not want his livelihood taken over by corporations. In the movie, he simply murdered his wife to inherit the farm. The book's title, *1922*, is suggestive of an era when modern industrialization began to overwhelm the old ruralism. The movie changed the story's message, because it is counterintuitive to the role of TV, which is surreptitiously to train viewers to conform. A man slaughtering his wife to gain property is good for TV, in terms of its message: "compete among your lowly selves to win money and possessions"—unlike resistance to corporations. Broadcasters are corporations.

193

Staples from yesterday's newspaper. These are in the news every day, they demonstrate that the newspaper is what I keep saying it is. Same staples every day? And no one is suspicious? On the front page, today's dead beautiful young person. Remember your life is pointless, folks! Inside, heroic accounts of the military (or police) and how they protect us from the forces of evil out there, and finally, the daily news could not be complete without the character assassination of a pervert [this time, actor Kevin Spacey]! Read all about it! Swallow this shit and believe you are nothing but a poorly paid employee handing over tax to fund our lifestyle! Believe utterly! Watch TV for even more!

194

I couldn't care less about the news but I'm aware that Robert Mugabe has been in it this week. Couldn't care less why. This pic of "Africans" celebrating means that whatever happened is enjoyable for the mega-rich owners of this newspaper and their friends so they decided to show happy "Africans" on the front page, just as yesterday it was a photo of Germany's Merkel looking as though she were about to cry over something, about which I couldn't care less but I understood from the pic that the story was distorted in favor of the newspaper owners' wishes. The other story on this morning's front page is an add-on slur against [car service] Uber. Uber is (was) a grassroots company that provided cheap, fine service to customers and allowed throngs of working class people to make some money. Therefore, the rich controllers of the country's wealth wiped them out and are finishing off the execution by slandering the memory of Uber, just in case another entrepreneur tries to make a similar thing. Job well done by the newspaper people and their controllers, The Establishment. Back to Mugabe in the news. Whatever's transpiring is in the interests of investors in Zimbabwe's resources who also own the newspapers. Why do I have to care what goes on in Zimbabwe? If I had to go there, for work, I would find out whether it is safe. But I don't. Take the biggest thing that everyone has been talking about for the last few years, Brexit. What is it? Everyone talks about it so seriously and it is just nothing.

195

Today's news headline is "Uber Leaked Personal Details of Fifty-Seven Million Customers!" How frightening is that. *My personal details!* Oh really? Like what? No one has robbed my bank account. Most [phone] apps, such as Uber's, login via Facebook. This is convenient for customers. If anything, Uber "leaked" (how and to where not stated in headline) only what I reveal on Facebook anyway—my name and city and some other trivia that makes no difference to me whatsoever. I couldn't care less. That's why I took no interest in the story despite I had the Uber app. The newspaper's loyal readers, on the other hand, are supposedly horrified and will say to themselves "I'm never gonna trust Uber again." *Fait accompli* by the old-money investors who saw off the upstart threat of Uber with the help of their accomplices who own the newspapers. For them, Uber had to go so they slandered Uber in the press and caused its collapse. I can similarly break down every news item and that is why I don't pay any attention to this twaddle. I'd rather read a good book and learn something useful.

196

Have you observed the recent rise of the middle-class pleb? I overhear them all the time (unfortunately). They seem to habituate Richmond in large numbers. White, over thirty, wearing office apparel and with an urbane southern accent, nonetheless they have the pleb mannerisms of a loud voice, know-all conversation revolving around work and buying stuff, and each utterance peppered with the F-word regardless of who can overhear. The middle-class pleb.

A.R.: Yep, they're everywhere.

197

This morning my iPhone informed me the fastest route to "work." Fucking thing monitors where I go every weekday and saves that as "work." Maybe traffic directions are helpful but I didn't tell Apple Corp. where I work. Anyway that's not my point. More pertinent is the core apps on iOS. These show Apple's vicious corporate vision for us consumers: "busy" workers preoccupied with money, appointments, keeping fit (to compete), and so on. Me, I'm just a failed musician who had to get a job.

198

What about if your early writings were known as "the juvenilia"—and so was all the rest of it!

199

Presently arriving in Dachau and you couldn't ask for moodier weather—just started snowing. Reck-Malleczewen died in the camp here.

No, there were a few [Nazi concentration camps inside Germany] such as Buchenwald. The ones in Germany were largely for Third Reich political prisoners. The genocidal ones were in Poland. Still tens of thousands perished at Dachau. I stood at the spot where Reck-Malleczewen must have met his end, not long before the camp was liberated, either shot against a wall or died of typhus (more likely) and his body buried in a mass grave nearby. Terrible end for a great thinker and writer. Feel like I went full circle today, in the footsteps of a man who lived in Hell and left a diary for no one.

200

Just had a weekend where I spent the whole time alone. Sitting in the pub *a cappella* now in fact. It's like the bad old days before I got the band together, say my first year or more after I moved back to England four years ago. Then, I just didn't know anyone. I couldn't call anyone and arrange to do something together. I spent every weekend on my own, both days. Eventually after about a year my friend from work Sev and I started going to the gym on Saturday mornings and very occasional nights out, before she moved away. I think I was numb with loneliness, and couldn't see any end to it. Music saved me. This morning I texted a female player from my soccer team politely asking if she knows whether we will be registering for the next league, which starts soon? When a woman has no romantic intrigue with you, she couldn't care less about you. No answer to a simple question like that. These little details are what define loneliness for lonely men.

A.R.: Sounds like a nightmare. Don't you ever meet anyone in the pub?

Do you mean someone new, meet in the pub? Never. It's probably because I don't go to any lively pubs. (There aren't any in Richmond.) During the bad old lonely days, I used to go to All Bar One or O'Neill's (both not the same nowadays), and would sometimes get talking to other customers, no one I stayed in contact. During the last three years, I made a bunch of great friends, a nice crowd of musicians mostly. What I'm saying is I don't lack great companions, including quite a few women, but I don't have a girlfriend, which makes me feel like Morrissey when "Two lovers entwined, pass me by...."

201

Had two intense flashbacks today, one at lunchtime and then another just now during the discussion of a pesto pasta. Earlier, I took a lunchtime stroll across Petersham meadow and the view of bleak empty fields took me back to my Shropshire childhood mainly because... I was freezing. A distant memory of being freezing cold on a December morning presented itself. That amused me because when you are a child you are dressed and whether those garments are adequate to keep you warm is beyond your reckoning, and all these years later I still can't judge how to keep myself warm! The other flashback was just a moment ago—I bit a pine kernel and was taken back to my university days when a combination of chronic poverty and anorexia made me fascinated with pine kernels—cheap, low-calorie food that could be nicked easily and consumed in carefully controlled measures. I re-glimpsed my twenty-year-old mentality, which was entirely prospects.

202

The stock response to "How are you" uttered across every shop counter all day long, "I'm good thanks" is bad enough but the one I really hate is in middle class, self-satisfied tones "I'm very well"—mainly because I always harken the missing word at the end: "off."

203

A species of *faux pas* unequalled in intensity of embarrassment is calling someone the wrong name, and this is not additive but multiplicative if you keep doing it (e.g., during a short conversation). For this reason, I can avoid calling someone by name for up to a year or more if I have any doubt.

204

Oasis made the music of my youth. All that Eighties punk and adored Sixties music is the sound of my schooldays. No one misses their childhood. What we look back on with heart-rending nostalgia is our youth—our twenties. Oasis is the music of my twenties. You might be able to find this online, I used to have it as a DVD, a brilliant "rockumentary" of The Beatles' tour Down Under. Utter mayhem. The Sixties generation never stopped saying how great a time that was to be young, and for me my hopes and dreams are forever linked musically to Oasis. That tune-thief Noel Gallagher lived my dream and, I guess, that of a lot of people. There was a famous magazine cover of Kate Moss naked under a Union Flag bedsheet, or maybe Liam was under it with her, and that pic captured my generation's dreams and fantasies, as did Twiggy to her Sixties generation. "Morning Glory" includes the lyric "Walking to the sound of my favorite tune" and that feel encapsulates my twenties, a big long sunny day.

London, January 2018

205

I always walk along walls and climb good trees. Recommend those activities.

206

After being "let go" by Synergy [medical communications agency] I was hired by another agency [ApotheCom] based in Westminster. The transition happened so quick I asked for a few days off in-between. This latest contract was supposedly that I write for a breast cancer account. During my interview I described my extensive experiences in oncology and breast cancer in particular and I submitted an example of my excellent writing. I got hired forthwith. That was three weeks ago. Once installed, I found out that the breast cancer account had not yet started. It still hasn't started. To fill my time, I was asked to look at some spreadsheets instead. At one point I was finding out drug names for EMA-licensed products. Those days dragged. Finally I was hauled into a side office by the… let's politely call him a nincompoop… who hired me and was told that my errors had made the company decide that I was unable to do the work. I bit my lip about my eighty-plus original articles published in major journals during my eighteen-year career at the top in med comms. So I'm currently seeing out my notice period doing odd jobs. The company told my recruiter that they were cutting my contract because I lacked the required skills. This is how these fuckwits go through life clinging to their jobs. Anyway, more contract offers coming in all the time.

207

They're all office employees who spend their workdays having meetings and warbling on the phone. A whole load of them do nothing. They're superb examples of evasive talkers whose everything is "on my to-do list" and "I'm going to start doing that next"—everything. I don't think they even fool anyone. If they're all doing nothing they stick together and cover each other. I was brought in to work (as a freelancer) on a pitch for a big project at a company [Virgo Health] in Richmond a few weeks ago. At first mind-boggling, I worked at it and broke it down into clear "do-able" tasks. After I had pretty much solved it, on a Wednesday afternoon (not even a Friday), the hiring manager suddenly told me that she herself was going to finish off my pitch, and that I was no longer required. I was dismissed. I am very sure she then took all the credit. I had literally no option, no one to turn to. I just had to walk out and not come back. My job over in an instant. That project hoisted in a million euros for someone.

208

The sports pages are almost as ruinous to your health as all the rest of your daily news. Look at this doggerel. I've mentioned it before, that the authorities are desperate to inculcate a love of sport in the taxpaying masses because of the wholesome values of competition—winning, defeating, prizemoney.... This particular piece, by the most boring journalist you will ever encounter, is designed to stop people thinking "Hang on, that goalkeeper is rubbish! How on Earth can he earn a fortune playing that badly?"—a disaster for the business owners in control of popular tastes.

June 2018

209

Two children (boy and girl) aged around three sitting next to me in pub absorbed watching Japan [World Cup soccer] game while eating ice cream. Senegal score. Girl asks what happened? Boy says Senegal just scored. I'm impressed. Girl says, who got the goal? Boy responds "Neymar!"

210

I remember [during soccer's Euro '96] cycling along Euston Road opposite Madame Tussauds coming home from work towards Camden and hundreds of England supporters were singing... maybe "Football's Comin' Home" and perhaps before the game where Gazza scored against Scotland? Our memories are unreliable. I only say my life and my memories are regardless of my "age"—the idea that I have a past that was nostalgic and irreplaceable and, somehow, a lesser present and disappearing future, I resent. I had a day today that must rank among my very best. Back in work after months laid off, so a massive relief. Plus, my contract was extended, and not one but three more job offers came in. From worried about whether I could afford to travel in to work, to having a choice of long, well-paid contracts. After work, which was fun and easy, I walked out into the brilliant sunshine and took the train to Richmond, met my wife-to-be and a few friends, saw France get through to the final (I bet £10 on them to win the World Cup before it all began), sat on Richmond Green for a while, then walked home to Kew with my betrothed. In what way was today not as good as whatever I did on this day twenty years ago? Age is a con. Like TV, the news, and all the other cons, it don't fool me.

211

Today I received an internal e-mail from a "User Experience Architect," whatever that is. This company (MRM Meteorite) is not an ads agency as such but designs "brands communications." It's replete with hipsters and fashionistas. Everyone's in shorts and a T-shirt or funky dress. It's fun. But the level of expertise is about as high as at a primary school. However, nowhere near as amateurish as Hive (ads agency I worked two years ago). There, the "creatives" simply extemporized medical knowledge. It took me a couple weeks to realize where they got all their misinformation—they made it up. (Treatments etc.)

212

At Synergy [previous workplace during 2017] there was a girl who was an office favorite due to being a hot blonde with specs whose routine was to be a bit goofy, very eager worker, despite lacking any remarkable ability (apart from deftly rearranging her hair). She attended each weekly meeting intently reading her portable laptop with looking up, giving a wave or giggle on cue whenever her name was mentioned. She was so gung-ho. This generation of young office workers is even more gullible than our group in the Nineties—the current crop are also prepared to work late, gazing at their laptops as their youth runs out.

I'm standing in Southwark Street texting this. I estimate that every person among the hundreds strolling past is an office worker fed, by TV and the news, the same propaganda which keeps them down and their lives impoverished.

213

I see things differently. All companies are places where the founder / CEO makes his great wealth by employing (literal meaning: using) people to work for him. Over time, the means that companies adopt to keep their employees working for the sole benefit of the CEO change, but the effect is the same. Nowadays, providing jam on toast, table tennis, beers on Friday ("Frinks"), and allowing employees to wear short pants are the minimal perks companies give their workers in exchange for using them for most of their life (five days every week) to make the CEO, and not themselves, rich.

If you ran a company with a hundred employees, would you rather splash out a few quid providing them "Frinks" and a table tennis table, or one million giving each of them a ten grand pay rise (when that million could be yours)? Table tennis, anyone?

214

The following hideous story will probably amuse you. A few weeks ago I espied in my local public house one of the young guys who (formerly) played in my soccer team. Although he had left the team a few weeks before, if I recognized him it's reasonable to assume he should remember me, right? So I approached him sitting at the table with his girlfriend who also used to play for the team (mixed 5-a-side) and announced hello. He looked at me with a complete absence of recognition and stutteringly offered "Er, do you know my mum?" and pointed to a plump old lady in their group. Then his girlfriend offered "Is it Alex?!" I said yes and turned to his mum and quipped "He doesn't recognize me with my clothes on!"

215

What about the deeply held conviction to self-righteousness of cyclists. I've been riding my bike to work using London's cycle lanes for the last few weeks so observing a cavalcade of cycle twats. They constantly make little remarks and utterances to other people as a way to communicate their self-righteousness. For example, when I slowed down to avoid colliding with a group of tourists who were idly dithering in front of me, the self-righteous twat cycling behind me gave me a little whistle and a tut, then rode through the tourists at full speed while shaking his head in despair. These cycle lanes have had two effects (apart from creating more twats). They have definitely reduced the hazard for being knocked over by a car, while substantially increasing the likelihood of stressful, unenjoyable daily encounters with twats and a hundred-fold greater risk of crashing with another bike. Cycling has gone from taking care to avoid danger from traffic to being forced to put up with aggressive assaults from other cyclists determined to undermine you. Cycle twats.

August 2018

216

You probably won't remember the circumstances of my dismissal from Synergy [med comms agency], but last February after a year of providing them with excellent service I got thrown out into the road and told never to come back. Then, in quick succession I went into two other agencies, which both gave me the usual mistreatment and chucked me out, and then I didn't secure a new contract for a few months until the present one, which I started a few weeks ago and will end on Friday. During those wilderness months, which ran from well before Easter till the end of the World Cup [April–July 2018], I took out a five thousand-pound loan which was all the money I had for around four months. Sounds like sufficient to live on, except when you remember my rent is a thousand per month and my regular outgoings five hundred on top of that. The loan just about covered those. Think how long you could last if you took home a thousand per month, and no one else in your household earned anything.

Needless to say, I ran out of money.

Then I started here [MRM Meteorite]. On my first day, I went to finances and told them I'm destitute, literally, have two mouths to feed and would they pay my invoices weekly. They agreed and added that all invoices are paid within fourteen days.

A month later, I'm still waiting to get paid. I've been down to finance department a few times to ask when I will be remunerated and the answer is always they don't know, payments are made externally and they can only send an e-mail requesting an expedient transfer. In other words, they pass the buck, and as soon as I walk out the room I simultaneously vanish from their concerns.

Here's what not being paid when my first invoice was supposedly due a couple weeks ago entailed for me. I could not pay my rent, again. My car payment did not go through. My loan repayment for the abovementioned five thousand was declined. My phone got disconnected (carrier: O₂, who have been robbing me with excessive overcharges for the last five years, cut off my phone for not paying last month's bill). Without a phone, I can't operate. I can't do anything. Both my banks constantly text and call me with messages to put funds into my account. As if I can conjure money. Both banks add on large charges every month.

During my past six years in the U.K., my singular experience has been to receive many impatient demands from creditors for sums that exceed the reluctant amounts dallyingly paid me by those who exploit my efforts.

September 2018

217

I haven't conveyed any good dreams lately but this one from last night is illuminating.

Background

Yesterday, because my rolling mixed football [co-ed soccer] league finished last week and the new league starts next week, I called the organizers to re-register with my usual team. The reply was, your usual team is not registered. Then he looked into it and said, actually, the players have re-registered as a different team without you.

I was shattered. I've played for that team for two years and consider the guys "friends" (of sorts), although I knew that two players who joined recently have been trying to take over, and I've felt a bit of hostility from them. I guessed those two had proposed to the others behind my back that they register as a team with yours truly *sans la nécessité*. I was... I dunno, saddened to say the least, and bitter about two people coming in and getting rid of me in such a sneaky way.

Last Night's Dream

It started with I was sitting at a kind of group picnic. I made a couple jokes that no one laughed. One of the jokes was my picking up (from the picnic blanket) something that was not a donut but could be mistaken for a donut, and I said "Anyone wanna donut!" and threw it into the air. It landed on someone's plate, who, like everyone else, did not find that funny. He was an old school mate from decades ago, not seen since—Ian Baker. Baker got up and dealt with another miscreant sitting round the picnic sheet. This was another person from back in the mists of time—Stuart Curle. Baker walked up behind Stuart and lifted him up by the seat of his pants (he was still in yogic *asana* position), then dropped him from above head height onto his backside. Stuart scrambled to his feet and they had a fist fight, Baker vanquishing him and leaving him lying in a heap. Baker then dealt with me. He came over to where I was sitting and likewise lifted me above his head and dropped me onto my backside on the grass. End of.

Interpretation

This dream is one of the most literal dreams I have had. I was "dropped" by my team yesterday and then "dropped" in the dream. Curley, the first victim of being dropped, tried to fight back and lost. Ian Baker was a boy who at school was known as "Bunter." More than thirty years ago and not remembered since. His nickname was Bunter because at football the most he could do, really, was kick the ball as hard as he could towards goal. Like the guys who have taken over my football team and ousted me, a similarity I can only make looking back after the dream. In the dream, I angered Bunter by clowning around in unfunny way and annoyed Bunter, and got "dropped."

Just like in real life. Stuart Curle was a hopeless football player at school and in the dream was dropped. My annoyance yesterday that my team had gone behind my back to form a new team was, to my reckoning, because there were too many players with the new additions and they decided to trim the team by ejecting me—the loner with the fewest friends. The dream tells me otherwise—my clowning around at the picnic symbolized "I'm not a serious team player" in reality (which is true) and I'm considered not useful by the others.

This dream helped me to realize the real reasons that I have been dropped, not my paranoid ideas that everyone hates me, more that I haven't worked hard enough for my place, which I can now appreciate.

218

In Japan one of my few true friends was Aussie James. He was a nearby neighbor and his kids (two girls) were age-matched exactly with mine. In fact I thought he was my doppelganger except for a minor thing, one day over lunch he announced "I'm turning fifty this weekend." I was shocked because I was not yet forty and I assumed he was around the same age. This means he must be almost sixty now. I haven't seen him since that part of my life was shot down in flames, eight years ago already. James is / soon will be my first mate to hit sixty.

How about that.

November 2018

219

Now you made me think about the puppet politicians who spend their lives talking and nothing ever changes. I noticed [U.K. prime minister] Theresa May does a little dance on TV nowadays and suddenly all the puppets have followed suit. Without caring one bit why they do this, I'm sure the dance is to signify how happy they are that they are winning votes or something like that. Anyway, I instantly had a flashback, to a line in Reck's [Reck-Malleczewen] diary where he despises the Führer for doing a little dance on hearing that France was defeated. So Theresa May has a political predecessor in Hitler.

220

Yeah it's my birthday at the end of this month. I couldn't care less about it. This follows on from all that I have been saying for years. I'm not something defined by other people who try to tell me "you are this" and if I'm impervious to cultural rituals (e.g. birthdays) then I originated in the group but decided to leave.

221

People grow old at different rates, can be in various phases of denial, and so on, but one uncanny age marker is this. I found it written on a sign in a park in Tokyo, of all places. Our age determines how long we can balance on one foot, with the duration declining as we get older. Reading the sign and the scale of how long I should be able to balance, in much scepticism I timed myself and, despite myself, a few seconds before my allotted time I began to wobble and collapsed at the pre-set moment!

December 2018

222

In the end, the parents [in the movie *The Glass Castle* about a highly dysfunctional family] were right. The kids all grew up level headed and stuck together for life. So that's the proof of the pudding. Throw in there that they were lucky as well. Their lifestyle invited disaster and they managed to scrape through virtually unharmed except the main girl's burns. Or maybe that's unforgivable enough. As for the dad, he reminds me of my Dad and myself as a father in a lot of ways. You can and should teach your children to be independent and know what's what. I myself have tried to build one glass castle or another since I reached adulthood—books and so on, and currently my own business which has swum sometimes and sunk at others.

My last night's dream was one of a long series of identical scenarios where I am searching for my door keys which I think are in a bag somewhere. I rummage through cupboards full of clothes and go from room to room looking for them. In last night's version I was in my brother's house (which was not his real house) with his kids appearing and saying something every now and then. This dream, which I have been having in one variation or another for years, screams out at me *how can I go home?* My brothers, like you yourself, successfully raised children in a normal family setup. I currently live in a small rented studio flat, no longer alone but with my new partner who opted to jump on board wherever my ship is going.

So back to the film. The dad was right in the end but he was lucky. What if he dropped the mom out the window and killed her during one of their drunken skirmishes? A dad in prison with the kids in care homes would have made a very different story. Look at my life.

223

Maybe it's an urban myth, but whoever studied how companies operate and likened them to the personality profile of a paranoid schizophrenic got it right. A typical experience (for me) is you are fired by a manager on the grounds that the company doesn't need you. Then you hear on the grapevine shortly after that that manager has left the company. You don't know whether he fired you because he himself was in trouble, whether he jumped ship for a better job, or simply doesn't care about anything.

Earlier this year I was hired for a month at an ads agency [MRM Meteorite]. Those people were fucking clueless. They knew nothing about medicine. They had one "medical specialist" a Portuguese woman who was a phony, smiling and pretending to like her co-workers. She had "meetings" all day long, was never at her desk. Anyway, she went on holiday abroad somewhere for two weeks. It was never confirmed, but because I was hired for a set period in advance, I think my assignment was to cover for her absence. At least, I was the "medical expert" while she was away, working on a lot of different projects, which were mostly crap, badly put together, and replete with mistakes. When the woman returned, I went through with her what I had done and showed her how a lot of the projects needed urgent repair. In front of colleagues, she said "Yes I noticed all these." So why hadn't she fixed them? Two reasons—not in her personal interest, and she had not noticed them. Needless to say, my contract soon ended and I never heard from that company again. A few weeks later, however, I learned that the woman left for pastures new.

As an "adult" let's say aged over thirty, rather than junior employee when in my twenties, I've only worked in medical communications so I don't know anything about other business sectors. But I can declare truthfully that med comms is overrun with morons. Those who are supposed to do the thinking have all got a science degree, not a medical degree, and because they have no imagination and zero capacity for work, they don't realize that their mathematical computer reasoning and career-led competitiveness are products of a very different mentality to that of an average physician, and especially a high-level physician-researcher who has spent a lifetime caring for patients. That is yet another reason that med comms writing by a young ambitious recent graduate is inevitably utter, unmitigated garbage and has zero chance of influencing medical practise or being accepted for publication by a professional peer-reviewed journal.

224

Just thinking about my time at Hive Health ads agency a couple years ago. Within a week or two of starting work there, I had alienated myself from everyone due to a glaring mismatch... I had some expert knowledge about medicine. They had a working system whereby a spreadsheet went out every Monday showing all the staff members' hours allocated to each ongoing project. Next to my name was nothing, every week. I probably only managed to get away with that untroubled because everyone knew I was a hired consultant, not a regular employee.

I had nothing to do, I never knew what I was going to work on every day I went in there (I was there for around four months). Usually I found something, but sometimes for days on end I had nothing to do! No one came to me or added my name onto their list of assignments. I used to write about things tenuously linked to ongoing projects. It was awful. The worry was, of course, that I would be inevitably booted out. This is my main memory—of hiding from my manager, Mel. I knew that she could only ask me to "step into my office for a chat about your future here" if she saw me. She was very elusive, the type of manager who just talks all the time, in endless meetings, so when she wasn't around I could relax. I used to enter the office in the mornings and the first thing I would check was whether she were at her desk. Finally, I got fired, by Mel, but she was actually humanitarian about it, and (this I know is true) she had rallied to keep me at Hive on several occasions, as the person who had originally hired me.

225

Think I just spoke to one of my old work colleagues from twenty years ago. In the line at Sainsbury's. Didn't realize till a moment after. It was one of those exchanges where you make a pleasantry then walk off in opposite directions, and then reflect, was that so-and-so? One of those puzzles where you take a picture of a young man and stick on cotton wool for gray hair, glasses for weak eyes, and a touch of pallor in the cheeks.

London, January 2019

226

My main aim this year is to eradicate going to the pub from my system. Pubs are for, and full of, losers. Only losers go to the pub! Pubs are full of timewasters drinking their lives away. I don't think anyone with any ambition in life ever goes to the pub. No one in the pub has anything better to do than waste their life. Just wanted to write those down.

227

I went to procure a morning coffee so while waiting, found myself flicking through the pages of that despicable rag *The Times*. One news story featured a French YouTube video concerning a protest movement, "Yellow Vests." Because I observed a bunch of similarly attired protesters holding up the roads on a couple occasions last year, I read the article. In not one sentence did *The Times* mention what the protesters are protesting. Instead, *The Times* rubbed in that they are "antisemitic" and called them "conspiracy theorists." Newspapers and their sycophant journalists are printed entirely to control the public's views. This story has ridiculed and thereby silenced a voice of protest and they did it because the protest is against the newspaper owners' interests, which are to preserve a status quo wherein they stay rich and have luxe lifestyles, several properties, world travel at expensive hotels, children at private schools, and so on, funded by the toils of a mass population of under-rewarded, taxpaying employees. So they can't allow those employees to think for themselves what's right or wrong.

228

What about a male employee with long hair who does an adequate job but doesn't realize his career is permanently on hold unless he gets a regulation haircut? My year-long unemployment during 2016 (hirsute) was immediately reversed when I had my hair cut short and then I managed to hold down my next job for an entire twelve months. That job only came to an end when it was decided that I was earning too much money for some people's liking so I was booted out and reduced to a pauper. If you wanna know why employees have to have the regulation haircut recall the myth of Samson and Delilah. In England you have one choice of a career. If you are a pleb and prepared to show your conformity by having a regulation haircut then you can be allowed uninterrupted, low-paid employment till you retire as an O.A.P. (Old Age Pauper).

229

Why would I repeatedly and consistently say for years that TV and especially the news is / are bad for your health, if I myself didn't really believe that and ignored my own advice? That would be very strange. We've gone over this one loads of times. I couldn't care less what TV controllers and news editors want me to think. C.O.U.L.D.N.T.C.A.R.E.L.E.S.S. What grownup people are told to believe is important is arbitrary and put there by people whose aim is to make you do what they want, for their benefit, not yours. I'm sure every man and woman in the country thinks that reading today's newspaper has done them more good than if they had read a good book instead. I disagree.

230

One of the girls in my office [Thrombosis Research Institute; TRI], I just overheard, told another one "Do you want to know an interesting fact I read today? Today, 01/29/2019, is one of only two days that have each digit of 2019 twice, the other date being 19/02/2019." Then they both walked out apparently accepting. I thought, what about 09/12 and 12/09? I am convinced that people will read and swallow anything, without ever questioning it or thinking about it. Just believe anything, especially in the newspapers or on TV.

February 2019

231

If you watch any Hitchcock movie or Carrie Grant movie or James Stewart movie from the 1950s, when they were going through their forties, it seems surprising now that those actors with graying temples were always cast as romantic leads versus young actresses. It's because the modern partitioning of people into "age groups" who cannot enjoy each other unless they knew the same pop music and culture from school is an invention of the TV Age, and as such, an artificial latter-day pronouncement.

232

You're forgetting the most important element—conditioning by TV and newspapers to think "I'm old." You know TV news is my favorite subject of vitriol. The most harmful TV is the least suspicious—comedy and sports coverage. I always hated comedy on TV—stand-up especially and "funny" personalities who host talk shows, all obnoxious and tend to trivialize their guests. Wogan was probably the only decent one, but he had the "TV" personality nonetheless. This persona acts as a watchdog of normality and is, indeed, the spokesperson of normality for TV viewers to suck up. Always conventionally minded, borderline numbskull but highly confident, they are TV puppets. Sports coverage (well, I only read football but it probably extends to all of it) is a microcosm of mind control for the dupes who swallow it. Indeed, a football team is a model of conventional normality and its goings-on an absorbing soap opera for the TV-opiated masses! A football team is above all, a workplace. There is the CEO, the boss, and the players who are the equivalent of company workers for real company workers to try to emulate. They work hard, give everything for the team, obey the boss (who is an elder while they are young).... A footballer is described as "old and reaching the end of his career" at thirty, and this trickles into the brains of news consumers. If you read the newspapers, they always give everyone's age. And then they paint a picture of that individual which reinforces a predetermined view of how they should behave at that age, and if there is a departure it is viewed as abhorrent or perverse, and inasmuch as the individual conforms to that pre-set design, then whatever they did is portrayed as normal behavior, even if criminal such as a tax evader and so on.

More importantly, how does one become an F1 driver? They seem just to appear out of nowhere. You can only drive an F1 car if, well obviously, you are an F1 driver.

233

"I'm teetotal. I haven't had a cup of tea all week!"

234

I wouldn't recognize him [TV personality Ricky Gervais]. I think you mentioned him before and at that time I really had never heard of him, but because of that I remember the name now. Why can't you accept that I haven't watched TV since the '90s, never read newspapers, and don't look at news on web sites. So yeah, I couldn't care less about "culture" on TV. I've been saying this consistently for twenty years. I don't own a TV. I don't read newspapers or look at news online. I'm not interested. I'm especially not interested in people who are famous for being on TV, making rubbish pop, or appearing in crap movies. So I make no attempt to find out about those. If you showed me pics of the twenty most famous people in Britain today, I'd recognize all the footballers but probably no one else. I have described my reasons for being not interested *ad infinitum* and *ad nauseam*. So of course I mean what I say.

Not watched *The Office*. I know what it is but not watched it. I access YouTube a lot but to locate stuff I want to watch. In short, I have not heard about and therefore tried to find "popular" TV shows, unless recommended by, well you, because no one else recommends me anything. Let's say people in my work were talking about the latest TV show and enthusing how good it is, and I overheard. The way they describe it would almost certainly make me have no compulsion to watch it.

235

If you wanna see clearly how devious are those sycophants the press, a good insight is to watch a game of football [soccer] and then read how it is subsequently reported, and note the inconsistencies. Then if you become convinced that they tell manipulative lies about something you can see for yourself, what does that imply about how they report other news where you can't see for yourself?

OK that was the preamble. Last year, the press decided to oust José Mourinho from his job as manager [head coach] at Manchester United. In a campaign that lasted a few weeks, all the newspapers (well, *The Times* is the one I read if it happens to be lying [sic] around), in unison began reporting every day "disgruntled fans at Man U," "boring style of play," "players don't want to play under him,"

"Mourinho must be sacked soon," and so on. I say above that what the press report and what you can see for yourself are inconsistent. I didn't see players refusing to play, boring football (or no different to normal), any of the things the press wrote. Inevitably, Mourinho was hounded out. Then, the press laid the boot in. The campaign switched to "Mourinho is yesterday's man," "his style of management out of sync with modern football," "no team would want to hire him now," and so on. Again, this did not fit my observations: Man U finished second last year, behind a phenomenal Man City, and achieved a number of points which any other year would have won the league. They also won the Europa league. Not a bad first year in charge for José.

The above would not matter if not for the following reason. During the last few weeks, the press have started again, this time stirring up a hate campaign to unpopularize the Chelsea manager, [Maurizio] Sarri. The tactics are identical: every day the back pages are reporting that the fans want Sarri out, the players don't want to play under his tactics, and that he must be sacked soon. My question is, how does the press know what players and fans are thinking? They simply make it up. And I predict Sarri will get hounded out soon, despite Chelsea doing okay.

Why Mourinho and why Sarri? My guess is this. Those two are the only managers I can think of who were not former players. They both drifted into football in later life and were tactically brilliant enough to become very successful. Indeed, Mourinho has, apparently, won more trophies than all the other Premiership managers put together. This seems to me an inside job, whereby the old-money men entrenched in a position where they can retire as a player and go on to have a very lucrative job as a manager, are closing ranks on their privileged status and not allowing non-footballers to enter the market and do a better job. And they do this in the same way that all very rich people who have a protected interest in preserving the status quo get their own way—they use their friends the press to stir up public opinion in the direction that they want.

236

I wrote the other day about how football [soccer] is reported in the news as yet another form of mind control exerted on people who read newspapers. A football team is set up as a workplace, basically. Something I forgot to add is that all teams fire their manager every once in a while. This is eagerly reported in the news because it makes readers think that getting fired is a normal part of life, and that they too are at risk of being fired if they do not perform according to the standards set by those who control their livelihood—senior managers, the CEO, investors, shareholders… in short, those who live well off the labors of workers.

One of the most oft-repeated bullshits uttered by senior managers to their subordinates, when trying to terrify them over losing their job, is "No one is safe in any workplace—even I could lose my job." This is bullshit. No senior manager has ever been fired. Why not? Because they don't do anything that could lead to a mistake in the first place. All they do is assign work to subordinates. They mostly pretend to be devoted to the company. They administer all the terminations to subordinates and are at no danger of being fired because they are always in favor with the CEO.

I also recently wrote that the press are trying to hound out [Maurizio] Sarri as Chelsea manager [head coach]. They're still at it. When Chelsea lost at the weekend it was all Sarri's fault, whereas the same was not said about managers of other teams who lost. Indeed, I have never seen any trial-by-press delivered against the managers of all the bottom teams, for example Huddersfield are having a nightmare, are rock bottom, and lose every week. The press have not said a word of condemnation about their manager. Moreover, Fulham, who are second from bottom and keep losing as well, are currently managed by press darling Roy Hodgson (who led England to lose against Iceland a few years ago) who is usually depicted in the newspapers as fighting a brave battle and other shit written about those in favor and who faithfully represent the virtuous values according to the press—working hard and so on.

237

We went to see Brentford F.C. vs. Anderlecht in a pre-season friendly that was so uninspired it was free to get in. However, the match contained an unbelievable highlight. Anderlecht had a corner, and kicked it not into play but over the stand and out onto the street.

238

You will never read a bad word in the press about the people who have all the wealth. I read Bonnie Prince Charlie's [Prince Charles] Wikipedia article today—a *coup d'etat* of disingenuousness obscuring that freeloader's exorbitant cost to us.

239

One thing I often ask when I go into my bank is "How much rent did I pay last month?" and to find out they always they have to scroll down laboriously through my statements. If it were a spreadsheet, it would be simple to sort the transactions into "payee column" and see all the payments to any particular payee at once. Why don't banks do this simple thing on our statements? I think I know why. They don't want us to see all their bank charges they themselves extort from us in one place. Better to hide them among all the other transactions. I say this because I went to pay my rent today and was told I didn't have sufficient funds. I said I should because I paid in one thousand the other day. I asked for a printed statement and left. It turns out I don't have funds because my bank (HSBC) helped themselves to two hundred quid "repayment" on a credit card I lost years ago. This suggests they have been extracting two hundred per month since time immemorial. I hadn't noticed because I don't even receive statements in the post and haven't checked my account online in years. And even if I did go online, I am not able to sort all my payments into each payee and see at a glance how much I've given them.

Now let's think. I haven't used my HSBC credit card at least since 2014. Why? After I started self-employment via my own business (in 2014) I found I generally had enough money to get through each month without using my credit card, which I only ever hitherto used to survive when I ran out of money. I stopped keeping a credit card on me and lost them years ago. I had around three thousand or maybe only two thousand debt on my HSBC credit card, not more. So how much have I repaid at two hundred per month for the last five years? Ten thousand pounds on an initial three thousand debt? I'll have to go into the bank and find out what's going on, but in all my experience of dealing with any bank or indeed any service business in U.K., I always receive disingenuousness from any rep, and usually leave not knowing any better. (Banks are the worst, followed by service providers, particularly O$_2$ and electricity companies.)

After a long arduous process I managed to extract info. Since February 2014 (a neat five years) I've paid ninety quid per month in repayments on my credit card. The reason it was twice that last week is because I missed a payment the previous month and got a double whammy. Maybe that is the sole reason I was alerted—until now my ninety quid instalments went unnoticed all this time. So to date I've paid five thousand pounds in minimum payments and have not reduced the initial "debt" (three thousand) by a single penny.

240

A.R.: Well everything we read is some sort of lie isn't it. Manipulation of the type you're talking about is just a bit more obvious. I think that virtually everything is made up to control us, but unlike you I still read and watch the news.

It's not that it's a lie *per se*. It's because it is a lie that is put there to make you believe something, or many things, or an entire belief system that keeps you *down*. I keep highlighting this. I couldn't care less if someone told me a fib. I do care when a set of people, the media, attempt to undermine my confidence and try to make me accept that I am an impoverished cog in a machine that keeps them rich and robs me of all aspirations. *Ibidem* my e-mails during the last twenty years, my message.

May 2019

241

Brilliant piece of wit from *moi*. Someone just said "Hey you!" and I ejaculated "Who's you, the sheep's mother?"

242

The human heart has only two powerful emotions—jealousy and envy. The more gifted you are, the more jealously you will claim your gifts. The less gifted you are, the more you will envy those of others.

243

When the news media began foisting women's soccer on the public by reporting it as though it were just as important and newsworthy as the men's game, they began by calling it "women's soccer." Now they have done away with that and indite "Arsenal forward so and so" "England captain Smith" and so on so that you don't know what you are reading till you click (on BBC web site) or start reading the newspaper. The news media maintain their coverage of women's soccer is "in the interests of equality" and nonsense like that. Or, "why shouldn't girls be able to play football as well as boys." This noble standpoint is, like all news, a load of bullshit. Someone stands to get even richer by having another sport bringing in more money. So they get their friends the news media to brainwash the public into liking it. All TV and especially news but also comedy and drama are only there for one thing—to keep you down. And that's why I have nothing to do with them! Comedy works by taking "normality" and showing how diversions from normality make you laugh. But at the same time reinforcing what you accept as normality. Drama works by showing "realistic" characters. They are realistic because they reflect notions of normality, and thereby reinforce those notions. Everything on TV is devised that way, by TV controllers.

244

My [vinyl] records (about three hundred albums with a quota of 12″ singles mixed in and up to fifty 7″ singles, all originals from '80s and a lot from 1960s, which I either bought second hand or appropriated from my Dad's collection) were all nicked from my garage in Camden around 1999. The thieves took those and left my car, which is kinda insulting.

245

I've been working on Kings Road for the last nearly one year and just observed, for the first time—indeed the first time ever—a Chelsea Pensioner. I was ordering a coffee in Gail's Café so I said to the girl serving "Do you know what that old man in the red coat is? No? A Chelsea Pensioner. They're war veterans." She looked utterly bored.

June 2019

246

I'm supposed to be not just mildly interested but "intrigued" to the point where this shit is the most important focus of my life! I can't think of anything more boring than news and nothing more harmful for your psyche than journalism. The same people (almost all adults) who declare "I don't have time to read books, *ho ho!*" read the newspaper and watch TV for hours every day. No one doesn't have enough time to read books. Just they have no interest in reading books. But they can't admit that even to themselves.

247

This journalist is a good contender for biggest twat [dishonest sycophant] in Britain. Check that first paragraph. Newspapers love sport above all, as the best way to keep you, dear reader, down in your lowly nobody place. Sports men and women are winners, unlike you.

248

He didn't notice that the lights had changed....

Today's historical investigation took your intrepid explorer to Redcliffe Square, scene of Guinness heir Tara Browne's 1966 fatal car crash, immortalized (if death can immortalize) in The Beatles' epic "A Day in the Life." The crashed car was at the site where the silver Peugeot on the right is today. The column to the left of the policeman is the one with 79 painted on it now, the next one along is behind the policeman, then there is a cluster of four columns and a bus stop still in the same place. Indeed, it was the bus stop sign in the very top right of the crash picture that confirmed I had the right location. The small sapling to the right of the policeman is now a large tree. However, the tree in the foreground (right of the car) is no longer there. There is however, a street lamp, which might have been put there in its place. In the crash pic it seems that the road was unlit at the time. The road still is, as it was then judging by the parked cars, a one-way street. This also confirms that the crash happened as he went through the red light. This road (stretching from Earl's Court to Chelsea) is a long, straight dual carriageway and it was reported that he was traveling over 100mph when the crash occurred, so possible on this road.

Incidentally we only think that Tara Browne was killed due to running a red light because The Beatles' lyric implies that. Actually, the lights are for a pedestrian crossing and the historical report was that he was the sole victim, his girlfriend also in the car was unhurt and no one else was involved. He crashed into a parked truck. The traffic light is immaterial and only really connected to our assumption that running a traffic light is dangerous, and Lennon's lyric. The real reason is he was speeding.

Chelsea is especially fertile for sleuthing because so historical. One street alone has blue plaques for Sir Alexander Fleming and Samuel Beckett and a house that used to contain the studio in which Nick Drake recorded all three of his albums.

August 2019

249

I just texted my Mom, regarding Spurs vs. Aston Villa, "This game has descended into bathos."

250

My definition of an old fool: Someone who believes unquestioningly in consensus reality after thirty.

Here are some common utterances made by old fools:

> "Money doesn't grow on trees"
> "What's on TV tonight?"
> "Everyone has to work you know"
> "I'm looking forward to my retirement"

251

[About Anthony Joshua] Never heard of him and couldn't care less.

Boxer right? I hate boxing and actually all sports, fixed cons designed to keep you down just like so much else put on. As I keep saying. I like football [soccer] because as a child I became good at it so I wanted to see if anyone else could be as good as me! Sports are *eidolons*—that word a gift to me from Walt Whitman—and I do not believe there is any such thing as "fair play" "rules" "competition" in the gullible sense, only this—rip off and you and I are ripped off forever.

252

The newspapers do all they can to encourage their readers, the people, to love sports. To the newspaper owners, encouraging a love of sports is akin to loving the values encapsulated in sports—hard graft, teamwork, sacrifice—all virtues the owners themselves never have.

253

I might not drink again, ever. Hard to pledge that one as "forever" but this time, unlike every other time I abstained for a bit, I don't have this yearning to go back or feeling of inevitability that I'll need a drink again down the line. This is really a novel feeling, that I don't want to drink again. Don't miss it or have any need for it. My former need was probably because of the social side (both drinking with friends and/or drinking trying to make friends) and de-stressing side. I don't need to drink for any of those reasons any longer. Indeed, they achieve none of those aims, more likely the opposite. I went with friends to Emirates stadium last night to watch Arsenal B-team run rings round my Brentford and the other guys were drinking beers while I had a Diet Pepsi. They did not become animated, boisterous, loud, or anything. They hardly changed and you would not have thought they had drunk a few beers each. It were as though we all had drunk three or four beers only or, alternatively, that none of us had drunk any beer. We all went our separate ways home after the game. This morning they probably feel slightly rough, whereas I don't. I had zero reason to drink beers last night, either to enjoy an evening with friends or alleviate stress, which I don't have anyway, apart from when I used to drink every night—stress, paranoia, and worry caused by drinking.

254

Because novelists, other types of writers, portrait painters, composers, musicians, and so on are collectively called artists it is assumed that they all do something essentially similar. Let's call it "creativity." This seems to me another broad misconception. Because although there are people who read books and people who never read books, and people who have no interest in "art" and have never entered an art gallery and those who do, there is no one who doesn't like some form of music. So I would place music as a separate category to other "arts" and call it "some primitive need for rhythm." And yes, the above people with no interest in books and art also listen to music that those who do like books and art consider unlistenable. I disdain the hypothesis that "each person has their own taste in music, and all is equal." Lichtenberg was correct: There is no such thing as bad taste, only good taste or no taste.

255

A woman will stay loyal to an image of a man as long as he remains impressive to her and likewise he will reciprocate to her as long as she supports him.

October 2019

256

My mate Henrik from Sweden asked me how come he's not allowed to WFH [work from home] whereas A., L., and K. are? I replied, favoritism. What about the nepotism in every office whereby all managers and their selected favorites (sycophants) are the only ones allowed to WFH?

257

Question for an astronomer. I was taught that the reason we have summer and winter is because for one half the year the Earth's tilted axis dictates we are pointed towards the Sun (summer) and for the other half away from the Sun (winter). I always doubted that. I thought surely as we went round the Sun, the top (or bottom) of the Earth would always point at the Sun? Anyway my question, if pointing slightly towards or slightly away from the Sun causes seasons, because when slanted toward we are slightly nearer, wouldn't a much greater effect be observed due to Earth's orbit being not circular but elliptical? I bet during perihelion (nearer) and aphelion (farther) those differences in distance from the

Sun are many times greater than the effect of the tilt of Earth's axis. Need to ask an astronomer.

258

You wouldn't expect a manufacturer whose history includes building personalized cars for Adolf Hitler and other Nazis, profiting from the Holocaust, and using concentration camp forced labor to be squeaky clean nowadays, but here's my experience of Mercedes Benz! When I bought my car (new Smart, a Mercedes marque) four years ago the clinchers were easy monthly payments, no road tax because of low emissions, and most compellingly Mercedes insurance which was £100 per year. However, after the first year, the insurance went up (not down) by a factor of five times to £500 per year! When I inquired why, their representative responded in corporate politesse "We no longer offer that insurance policy." They did not say "We only offered that to rope you into buying the car knowing all along we would revert to expensive insurance after a year, sucker."

Then I hardly had anything to do with Mercedes till this month. The terms of my buying the car are, I pay monthly instalments for four years then at the end of that period (now) I can either pay off the remainder (about half the original price left), part exchange it for a new one, or return it. I want to keep it so I selected that option and asked them to set me up a financing agreement whereby I pay off the rest in thirty-six monthly instalments—similar to what I have been doing for the last four years (paying them money), miraculously not being late once.

What they replied in corporate parlance, is "Our underwriters will need to do a credit check on you using 'Equifax.'" Because I know this is a disingenuous company that operates in a country (U.K.) where all companies more or less are disingenuous and where customers expect no less, I knew this mention of some semi-believable external "credit score" check meant there's no way they are going to let me pay off the car in monthly instalments. What they really want is for me to buy a new one. That's all they will allow based on they know that nobody who buys a cheap car on monthly finance has six grand handy to buy off the final payment.

Naturally, the outcome of that was "Our underwriters have declined the refinancing option based on the credit report conducted by 'Equifax.' If you would like to know the reasons, you may contact Equifax to request your credit score."

Needless to say, Equifax web site mentions nothing about how I can find out about what they might have said about me and in fact I couldn't care less and don't believe there was any contact between them and Mercedes or indeed that any company can investigate my finances like that. Or that there's anything particularly wrong with my credit given that I managed to get a loan as recently as last year when I was penniless. Why didn't Merc investigate my credit history when they sold me the car on the spot four years ago?

I also knew that they would pretend that an independent organization who are nothing to do with them would be imputed to have made the decision, not themselves, so as to preserve an image in my mind that they are lovely people and not to make me resolve to go buy a new car elsewhere.

Lastly, during the recent correspondence about all this, they have introduced a new terminology for the first time! My monthly repayments on the car have changed from being monthly payments to "rentals!" They have suddenly started saying "Your last rental payment for the car will be in October." They have not used that term till now. This must be to make me believe that I have been renting it all along and now is the time to give it back.

I can't think of a single openly honest company and no more than one in ten persons in their work capacity who can talk truthfully and give a straight answer in U.K.

259

People are sometimes uncertain about whom they fancy but always know whom they don't. Therefore if someone is uncertain whether they fancy you, they do.

260

You watching England [soccer game on live TV]? Some kinda orchestrated disturbance going on....

Took me around twenty seconds to realize what they're doing, with actors staging a mass exodus at the pre-set moment. TV manipulation at its best! Obvious propaganda. A typical mass deception *à la* TV. Am I the only person who can see that everything on TV is bullshit? How anyone can watch TV and keep a straight face amuses me endlessly.

261

[Next day after the above] I wanted to see how the press would react to last night's mass deception—whether there might be some doubt or a torrent of support to back up the lie. Pic attached. To understand what happened last night, you need to know the background to the game. Basically, Bulgaria's stadium was half closed (you saw all the empty seats) as a punishment against their supporters causing trouble against another visiting international soccer team a month ago. Indeed, they are traditional ethnic rivals from that part of the world. The ensuing commotion was labeled "racism." The other point was that all last week, the U.K. press and TV news built up an image of Bulgarian fans as "racist" (for the gullible masses to swallow easily) and asked what would the England players do if subjected to racism? Would they walk off the pitch? The football authorities dutifully devised a "three-step stop the play scheme." So the stage was set to try it out. All they needed therefore was some racist fans just in case none showed up. The ground was half closed don't forget. Oh, and those allowed in were recognized official fans. Oh, and identified troublemakers already banned (none of this will be mentioned by the liars who write newspapers). So, they went out and hired a bunch of suitable people to stage a disruption and dutifully walk out when the game was halted (right on half-time so as not to interrupt the match really). On TV, they looked like students all wearing the same hoodie. They did not have the fat beer guts, tattoos, ugliness, and generally a bit older appearance of real troublemakers. And a group of racist hooligans that large would not voluntarily walk out I'm very sure. It's hard enough to chuck out a lone troublemaker usually, even at Brentford F.C.!

So the whole thing was staged, only pretended to be real. That's my objection to news, treating me like an idiot who will believe anything. And who therefore can be manipulated and kept in my place.

Any minor objection to my version of events outlined above can be explained within it. For example, why would the football organizers do that anyway? Easy. The old men who make huge salaries at the FA, UEFA, FIFA [soccer governing bodies], are all white faces while those on the pitch are all different complexions! So the old white men have to pretend they care about racism. As if not allowing supporters to chant abuse at footballers will cleanse their minds from all evils.

Right that's enough about that. You know what I think about TV and the news and if you still doubt me then there's nothing more I can say.

262

… another objection might be why would Bulgarian organizers agree to go along with the hoax? Well take a look at their half-closed stadium. UEFA [soccer authority] could have said "The stadium will be maintained sub-capacity for the next several games unless you agree with us to take further steps (last night's performance) to 'tackle racism'—and if you do then we'll allow you to re-open your stadium (i.e. make lots of money)." That should work.

263

I said the "racists" were planted there. They'd be pretty unconvincing planted racists if they behaved nicely. They were planted there and told what to do. In the footage you can espy them chuckling as they sheepishly make a feeble Nazi salute. The players on the pitch had nothing to do with the hoax, they were duped like everyone else. I'm in pub now—all the gullible plebs are in here saying "Did you see that despicable racism on TV yesterday? And their manager pretended not to hear anything! Bulgarian scum!" Er, aren't you being a racist now?

264

Patrolling down Kings Road now. The regulation short-all-over haircut paraded by every man in Britain is a telltale sign of a people terrorized by fears for their job, their safety—all thanks to their steady daily diet of scaremongering on TV and newspapers. Bunch of wimps! This country has the most revolutionary past of any other nation—the Barons Revolt, Peasants Revolt, Magna Carta, Glorious Revolution, English Civil War... now I'm the only revolutionary left.

265

More manipulation [a TV news report about racism in soccer]—probably a desperate attempt to retain credibility amid feedback that last week's fraud was one of the most amateurish attempts to hoodwink everyone that not only did I see right through as it happened but also others must have suspected something amiss. Every football fan who attends matches has seen troublesome supporters ejected and this didn't look anything like that. So this latest report is designed to deflect away from people realizing the whole thing is a farce. I can summarize all TV and all news media in a simple formula. "There exists a status quo whereby rich people control via their wealth the ninety-nine percent of other people who do okay or not at all okay, in order to exploit them and thus increase their own wealth. The rich people own and control all the news media, and hire the right types of journalists and actors to broadcast out to those who do okay or not okay what the rich want them to see, hear, and think."

266

British Bullshit Corporation.

267

Have you seen a fox this year? I haven't. Not one. Prior to this year I saw foxes practically every day—usually dead in the roadside but also commonly wandering the streets at twilight. When an observation goes from "every day" to "never" it arouses suspicion. My conspiratorial mind goes like this. Impossible to prove, but when a species becomes extinct it's usually because of human activity. I wonder whether rich people decided that having their bins rummaged and the occasional bloody vulpine corpse on their Bentley could not be tolerated any longer and they demanded via their channels of obeisance that this must stop. As we know, the rich have always hated foxes. And so their agents, let's say police, poisoned them all. No more London foxes. And this can never be reported, of course, because of any possible outcry from horrified commoners. Although even so, that would not lead to any reprisals, of course.

268

The direction we're going so far, this century will be remembered as "the unartistic, musically bereft period of clueless drones."

269

Remember I mentioned recently that the present era is (so far) "the unartistic century"? This is further reflected by all the great living writers whose books awed me in the 1990s haven't written either anything at all or anything great during this century. These include: Camilla Paglia, Stephen Dobyns, Paul Auster, Brad Leithauser…. All had a fairly prolific output in the '90s and have written only worthless bits or nothing since then. (Paglia possibly excepted with the excellent *Glittering Objects*.)

Back to my initial question. Are there periods in western civilization where languor and un-inspiration seize everyone, and are we going through one of those now?

270

Yes and yes back. Except I say that the whole of '70s music including punk was a tired-out response to the '60s. No music made in '70s was unthinkable a decade earlier. Early Clash recordings which were supposedly "revolutionary punk rejecting all that went before" could have been on *A Hard Day's Night*. Except The Beatles sang Love and Peace while The Clash sang Hate and War. Same melodies and same instruments. And The Clash harmonized just as heavenly as any '60s band. Even punk-style lyrics had been done by the end of the '60s. I bet if you Google "first use of F-word in pop record" it'll be '60s.

The real change in music post-'60s came along for the same reasons that the '60s occurred in the first place. The '60s were caused by the invention of electric guitars and the next truly innovative music followed the invention of another new instrument(s): synths and drum machines (computer instruments). And so '80s music was entirely new. Even '80s guitar bands played a new-sounding music—chiming arpeggios from the likes of Johnny Marr and the Edge.

It'll take an unpredictable novel(ty) instrument to cause a new kind of popular music. Something not invented yet.

November 2019

271

Last week a "baller" [soccer player] (Xhaka plays Arsenal F.C.) "disrespected" (newspaper talk) his own fans! Now it's time for journalists to do their job. Their function is to preserve the status quo whereby their masters, the very rich, can go about fleecing ordinary people unobserved. So the spin doctors are repairing this rich brat's reputation with a sob story about how his "state of mind" was "under intense pressure." The ploy is to remove any real attention on a player and restore him as a "people's hero who gives everything for the team." Then the plebs will forget about any interruption to their normal lives of working for a minimal salary one third of which goes to Her Majesty, one third to their landowner, and the rest can just about afford a single thing to look forward to, maybe watching Arsenal but probably only on TV.

272

Today's dead beautiful youngster given the front page treatment. These newspaper magnates, news editors, and journalists should be summarily shot for how they invade people's tragedies and twist gullible readers for their own ends in service of their masters, the rich.

273

Just, looking around me, I'm incredulous that every-single man has the same short haircut. No exceptions. Fifty years after the Sixties, you'd have thought there would be equal proportions of any hairstyle you can think, with people saying "This is how I individually choose to have my hair." Instead, everyone has the same, most boring haircut there is, which is the army-grunt haircut. And it is accompanied by the blandest society I can ever remember. And nearly everyone you encounter is a pleb or, if a bit more refined, just docile.

A.R.: You can't help being bald though.

December 2019

274

Don't often get to hear TV commentators cos I normally watch football [soccer] in pub. Commentary on at home now. I worked out commentators long ago. There are always two of them—one authoritative main commentator with a commanding, well-spoken British accent and one excitable, northern English or Scots sycophant. The former describes what's going on during the match and intersperses that with knowledgeable anecdotes. For example, "He made his Premiership debut here and on that occasion United were the eventual winners in a memorable game that included five goals." Or "He spent three seasons earning his living in France, at Lyon." You name it. For these, he has a list of pre-scripted quips researched by TV people who do that sort of thing. Whenever any player gets the ball, the commentator has an option to drop an "off-the-cuff" so-called (so it sounds) piece of expert knowledge. With each, he crosses it out lest he forgets and accidentally repeats himself later. This trick gives the impression that not only do broadcasters know everything but also that everything about football is essential knowledge. Meanwhile his sycophantic sidekick's job is to get over-excited with contributions along the lines "How did he miss that? He must be cursing himself! A player of his quality doesn't often miss chances like that! He'll be disappointed with that." As you can see, they have all sides covered. Everyone listening hears some TV bullshit.

275

Did you watch the football [soccer] on TV last night (with commentary)? I was laughing the whole game—all the commentators do is one of the duo (the superior type) mentions off-the-cuff pretend-knowledge while the other (the sycophant whose job it is to tell viewers that these players are "quality") feigns over-excitement at the unfolding action. A mainstay of this TV formula is the (scripted) conversation piece between the commentators. The front-man tells the audience "It was at this stadium where City began their campaign last season." Then the sycophant (following the script) joins in "I remember. It was a tough match." (Camera zooms in on a player warming up) "And on that day it was this man who scored the vital opening goal." "Ah I remember, fine finish with the left foot." Television can pretend anything is real! Even a so-called improvised conversation. That's because everything on TV is bullshit, all designed to keep you down! I've said a lot about sports journalism over the years. It's just as dangerous for your health as all other news. For example, why is it necessary to have a sycophantic commentator on every game? ("He'll be aiming to use his quality to get on the score sheet this afternoon!") Listen to the sycophant next game you watch. It's sickening. Why is he on TV? That's easy. Unless the TV audience is told that the players are superstars, some viewers might think "Why do footballers get paid what I earn in a decade every week? That can't be right. Wait, and why do other rich business types take home even more than that? I feel angry now. That's not just!"

276

Now watching United with commentary on. Rashford earned a penalty. Before he took it, a few minutes ago, the commentator proclaimed "Rashford has had a mixed record on penalties this season: so far it has been score, miss, score, miss, score, miss." Within less than a minute later, Rashford scores the penalty. The same commentator utters "Well there could be little doubt that Rashford would hit the back of the net!" They forget what they say—as do the TV audience. Tonight's sycophantic co-commentator (a barely comprehensible Scottish moron) is magnificently obsequious and sickening.

277

If you're not an office ass-kisser, let's say like me you can't do it. I just can't do it. You accumulate minus points. Let's say someone in senior management announces something even more ludicrous than usual. Ass-kissers will all nod eagerly in agreement and say that's a really good idea. Every time that happened and I didn't say anything, the senior will have noticed and awarded me one minus point. Eventually you accrue sufficient minus points to get yourself fired on the grounds of hatred.

278

For this Tory rag's [*The Times* newspaper] contents, they hire a self-satisfied, opinionated windbag like this buffoon and let him write what he likes. The desk editor then checks that his day's hackwork follows the Tory rag's party line and promotes its values—cementation of the status quo and promotion of the good image of businessmen. Same with all news media—everything they print or say is tinged with manipulation.

Midfielder is full value for £63m price tag despite City's faltering start, writes **Paul Hirst**

Many footballers...

279

"Century of the Businessman"—Maybe that's what's happening now. I couldn't care less about elections, politicians, and the news but I noted that the Tory-Times published a map of Britain this morning that was almost entirely blue with some red bits at the top. Maybe with all the precariousness of this century's first twenty years, which began with a memorandum that rogue people could crash hijacked airplanes into us, everyone just wants some return to feeling safe.

A.R.: So… do you mean you're uninterested to the point where you don't know the outcome of the [U.K. general] election?

Yes. Except that when there's something that everyone around you is talking about you can't help but overhear bits. If I had the day off work yesterday I doubt I'd have known there was an election, and if I had the day off today I wouldn't know who won—nor would I try to find out, because I'm not interested.

If you barged into your next-door neighbors' house and listened to them talking about what they're planning to do over the next few weeks, months, or years, it would be a bit out of place if you tried to interrupt and tell them "Don't do that, do this!" And that's what politics is to me—a bunch of people talking, not listening to what I might want, and not even certain whether what they say will turn out. All they do is talk. It has nothing to do with me and I'm not interested in anything they talk about. I hate Tories and I love Europe. However, I think we are stuck with Tories and soon out of Europe? Politics has nothing to do with me.

280

The Mantra of the TV Watcher:

I'm so moronic, I'll believe anything!
Show me what to believe, and I will!

[Inspired by distant memory of *Songs of Innocence* poem by William Blake, "My Sweet Joy"]

281

I read an OK-book the other day titled *Three Types of Solitude* by Brian Aldiss. It was one of those inexpensive miniature paperbacks with less than a hundred pages, a lunchtime book. Not one of those three short stories rang to my ears anything like solitude. I might write a rebuttal. I'm now watching Chelsea F.C. on TV at the (bachelor) flat of my good mate Peter who is eighty years old. I expect he knows a little bit about solitude. Meanwhile my partner Natasha is sedated in a ward in hospital. She's in her own solitude. And lastly there is the biggest hermit of them all, *moi*. Three types of solitude.

282

If anything, I try not to think about the time of year, what year it is, or whether the weather! I'm just here and alive today. It's the only way I found my quietus. Happy Christmas!

London, January 2020

283

When I moved from Shropshire [in the British Midlands] to Milton Keynes [city just outside London] as a young teen in early Eighties, I was a country bumpkin! I was embarrassed about my Brummie-toned accent and went about losing it. I'd never been on a bus before. One day, after school, I hopped on the bus with a big bunch of other kids. I went to pay the driver, but he waved me onboard. After we set off, the conductor came round. He asked me where's my ticket. I said oh it's okay the driver let me off. Blinking incredulously he said what, don't they teach you anything at school? I saw the whole bus was laughing. I am still the same, different.

284

Movers 'n' Shakers

When news media such as *Time* magazine and so on compile lists of "The 100 Most Influential People Today" what they hide is the fact that those chosen people are only influential because the news media made them influential and indeed spread their influence. What those people truly are, are persons whose values coincide with those of the media. The only movers and shakers are the media.

285

[Killing Joke guitarist] Geordie is the only person ever to play that guitar [Gibson ES-235] properly—although in a way that the 1940s / '50s inventors never would have imagined. No other hollow-body guitarist has attempted to use that particular guitar, which is a bucking bronco of feedback and other idiosyncrasies, making it perhaps the most difficult guitar. All the other semi-hollow guitar *maestros* from Scotty Moore and The Beatles to Johnny Marr and Oasis went for the Epiphone Casino, which is half as slender and much more manageable.

February 2020

286

Watched good documentary about the Nazis last night (*World War II in Color*). Was just musing on one of my favorite quotations from A.J.P. Taylor, re: Might Is Right. "The Nazis had been imposing their view of what is right over other Europeans since 1940. They themselves were about to receive the same lesson from the Americans—might is right." The Nazis wanted *Lebensraum*, "room to live in" for themselves. This coming century, we might reach a world population of ten billion and the issue of *Lebensraum* could re-emerge—who will have space to live? Then, once again the strongest takers will proclaim "Might Is Right."

287

Was in hospital visiting Natasha earlier and since a TV was on I caught a bit of nightly news-propaganda. This was about coronavirus. The news item was "Brits Quarantined on Luxury Ocean Liner Held at Japanese Port." It didn't say which port. It showed an aerial view of people walking on the ship's deck and cut to shots of ambulances. The propaganda narrative went "Some Brits quarantined for their own safety aboard ship." They are allowed to exercise and receive medical attention. The propaganda message is "Japan is safe." Then the TV action cut to China. Meanwhile, the Chinese are rounding up anyone thought exposed to this virus and shutting them down. The scenes are merciless Chinese military pushing civilians along prison-like corridors. The contrast is meant to imply "Well we've shown that some Asians (the Japanese) are all right but don't forget most of them (the Chinese) are wicked barbarians."

So—the Chinese not only round up and isolate to perish their infected cases but also they film that and show it on TV. Hmm. Why would they do that? To show that they are defeating the virus? Nope. They're not that stupid. If that were the point they would show humanitarian doctors treating the wounded with plenty of white isolation suits to represent that it is contained and controlled. Not brutality. If China did indeed harshly imprison infected individuals (which they might), they would cover that up. So who were the prisoners shown on TV? I don't know. Could be anyone. It's propaganda and you all watch it! And believe every word!

288

A.R.: Maybe there is no virus?

That's precisely at the point of why I don't watch TV. To me at least, there is definitely no virus, no Brexit, or anything else. I only have my life. I couldn't care less about anything else. All TV does is keep you scared and keep you down. It's a con, just as rich people and poor people is a con.

289

Natasha been in hospital and, even though the bosses are aware of that, [my employer] TRI has canceled my contract so I'll be back jobless, and we'll be broke, in April. Stuff like that. Oh, and I think I broke a metatarsal playing football last night. Can't walk.

I was just hobbling towards a local café and clearly had a head-start on two chavs also approaching, but because I'm limping they increased the pace and nipped in the door then stood in front of me in the line, chatting together about the news and stuff. There are just chavs everywhere. These are the two phrases I detest the most in cafés: "Can I get" or "I'll have…." Apart from those, loudmouth plebs everywhere can't say more than five words in a sentence without using "like." These people all flourish in their jobs and I can't hold down a contract for longer than a few months. Yes I'm fed up.

I texted work to say I've got a suspected broken foot and will need to go hospital to get it checked, and the response was "I have informed your manager."—Not are you all right? Nothing.

March 2020

290

A.R.: This is propaganda at its most powerful. This morning TV news had "mass epidemic countdown" written across the screen. The word pandemic is starting to be used all the time too.

I've been saying and writing along those lines for years. I've said that all TV and news are irrelevant to me and I don't expose myself to any of it. The only way not to be controlled by TV is the same as anything else that's bad for you—don't touch it.

291

Keep the Workers Distracted with Constant New Fears!

Two work colleagues and I went to see *Colors From Outer Space* (Nic Cage's worst-ever acting) at Prince Charles Cinema Leicester Square last night. After the movie, SoHo was for once eerily deserted. Because I'm not saturated by fears propagated on TV it didn't occur to me why—but the other two remarked "No one wants to go Chinatown because of worry about coronavirus." TV is so effective at promulgating fear that the entire population can be made irrational by their addiction to it. They would rather watch TV and be overwhelmingly preoccupied by what's shown on it than think: "Why do I spend my whole life working for peanuts when one third of my income goes to rulers who do nothing and another one third to a property owner who also does nothing except keep tabs on what I owe him?"

292

All the worried sheep are locking themselves in their pens with only their TVs to bring them news of the outside world! Streets empty. I just went Maids café. When I walked in, an elderly woman wearing literally a Darth Vader respirator shouted "Stand back! You have to stay two meters apart!" Old man leaning over the shop counter was bellowing commands for service, as though on a battlefield. These people are truly panicked. I said to Kimberley the owner, everyone nicely wound up in here! To which she responded anxiously, you can't be too careful! And ran off. We're working from home (WFH) this week.

293

Sitting in an empty Micro Beer [liquor store], Sean the owner listening to government puppet official pledging "income for all disrupted businesses, mortgage holidays, full support for all those affected…." Meanwhile, I still have to face unemployment next week (due to government changes in tax laws) with no let-off of my forthcoming VAT, corporation tax, etc. So I'm the only person fucked in the country. Kimberley from Maids café was distraught today about "threats to the loss of my livelihood." As an old friend, I automatically went to give her a don't worry hug—which made her jump away with fright. Of course, TV has warned her not to touch anyone. She'll get through this intact. I'm the only person who's fucked. Another thing everyone is parroting today (which means it was on TV) is "The whole world is changed forever now." That alone tells me how much this has been blown out of proportion by news people, and really should be a reassuring suggestion that they do know better and that this will certainly pass. Apple News headline was "U.S. Adjusts to New Reality." My manager (in States) earlier mentioned something about "the new way of life." So this is the next thing for the masses to parrot about. As though the arrival of HIV forty years ago didn't have any effect on changing human life.

294

I was marching across Kew Bridge yesterday early evening when I heard my name called—cos of my terrible eyesight friends always see me before I see them. Katy and her boyfriend suddenly standing right in front of me. So I reached out with the customary hug—causing them to recoil with a pirouette backwards. That was the first time I learned that TV had issued a *fatwa* that people must not touch one another.

295

This might amuse ya. Just sent it to couple mates at work who interested in movies so we occasionally watch together. They seem a bit nervous about my so-called quarantine (WFH) imposed on me this week.

> Sat sounds great. I'm fine. I been saying for years, please don't watch TV. It's not good for you. It is purely designed to keep you down. If you guys wanna see me on Sat, invite me along. If you're worried and don't, I get it. I been isolated all week, have you? Think about this. In 2000, every product imaginable was available in brick mortar stores. Now everything is online. Companies noticed that renting a space to show their products wasted money versus the internet. I tell you that the rest of industry is catching up. Why do we all need to sit in an office when we could all WFH? This virus scare has led every company to transition to WFH. Have you heard a new expression all week "the new reality" "the new way of life"? This whole thing is businesses getting everyone to work home from now on. Offices will disappear — but not low-paid employees! I tell everyone — avoid TV and newspapers. All they do is bring you down. See ya on Sat !! 21:18 ✓

One of the—well actually, the only—comical aspects of not following closely (on TV) the covid-19 hoax is I never know what stage of the hoax we're at! The other day I was still going to hug people (friends who shrank in terror) and this morning I innocently went into Maids café (the door was open and people were inside) when a frantic employee screamed at me "Wait outside! We are adopting emergency procedures!" So I walked to the next café, on Kew Green. There, the door was similarly open wide and emblazoned a sign saying "Takeaway only" with all tables barricaded. Don't get me wrong, I'm all in favor of a rational, scientific response to a threat to human health and I comprehend that that is the basis of what we are seeing. What I don't like is the groundswell of underlying bullshit that comes with this TV-spouted nonsense, namely these new buzzwords "the new reality, the new way of life." Sorry, western society has survived intact for centuries without a few reporters on TV telling us, with one week's notice, that we have to live differently now.

"The new reality" is perfect television for the TV Age, and tells me that this is all orchestrated. It's the biggest hoax since 9/11. And like 9/11, the perpetrators are untraceable and unaccountable. Because the same people. The powers who control the world's wealth. What is this disease petrifying everyone that no one has or has seen? A hoax. Why then? Because I'm the only person who is ruminating about it, I expect I'm ahead of the pack as usual. Just as 9/11 was devised to get around the illegality of staging a war against not another state with an army, but an ideology ("war on terror"), this little *putsch* seems to me devised to change the way people work, and that's it. Why? It's something along the lines that westerners are becoming redundant in our own created world. We're too expensive. Outnumbered by billions of Asians who'll do everything for a fraction of our cost, we're becoming unemployable. Redundant. The people who run the world must be thinking how can they keep cutting costs both to preserve their vast wealth, and keep industrialists the dominant culture on the planet? WFH [working from home] stared at them in the face. They considered "How can we make every business undertake that, all at once, and make every employee agree to conform at the drop of a hat? It would take something like a deadly disease outbreak to make everyone too scared to go out." So that's what they planned to concoct.

297

Covid-19 is perfect news because it incites mistrust and segregation among the population—an evergreen theme and desired aim of businessmen-controlled TV.

298

Très prescient of Sainsbury's.

299

Yesterday, my work [Thrombosis Research Institute; TRI] had its first virtual online meeting for all team members prior to transitioning, next week, to WFH for all. Don't forget, I had already been banished to WFH due to scaremongering (when I innocently reported I'd been under the weather a few days ago). I tuned in from bed. Each person had to say hello on shared screen and report what they were doing. They were all still in the office. When it came to my moment, I appeared on everyone's screen and announced with a smile, "Rumors of my demise have been greatly exaggerated!" This was met not with a single expression of acknowledgment but only with icy daggers of hatred from senior managers.

Why? Because of the frivolity. The SMs were all preparing to weigh in with speeches about the long-term "new way of life" and earnest statements that (quote) "As one family, we will provide you every support as you move into the new reality." Hmm. If I'm family and the only person quarantined so far, why can't anyone ask whether I'm alright? And why fire me next week, when possibly no one will be hiring any stranger for the rest of this year or longer?

300

Clues include what those disreputable connivers the news media have been doing today. Don't forget, all they do is lie to you, fool you, and manipulate your thinking so that in the end you can't think for yourself. Let's say that faced with not being able to finish the [English soccer] league, and after feverishly calculating how every combination of alternatives affects their investments, the controllers decide to void the league, as the best settlement for their money. Now all they have to do is announce it. For that they need skilled manipulators. "Get us the BBC!" First thing to do is soften the blow on football fans by picking on the weaker lower leagues for starters. They're voided. Done. Now wait a few days for everyone to accept that before announcing the Premier League also. This morning, on BBC Sport website, appeared a saccharine memory of when the league was last voided—this was before it was announced that non-league would be voided (which was announced an hour ago). Manipulators like to use steps of information release. So this morning they put together a soppy reminiscence of previous times when the league was voided. The headline was "Through war, terrorists, hard times, we as a Nation have always pulled through, together!" Then the story followed: WWI... WWII... a really cold winter in 1963.* (No terrorists or any other incidences of when the nation all stuck together were related.) That piece of hack journalism was hastily put out so as to prepare everyone for the announcement that the Premier League is to be voided, as revealed in stages so as not to cause a riot.

---

*Actually, the football league was not voided in 1963.

301

The most harrowing thing [about covid-19 hoax] was the appearance, everywhere, all at once, overnight, on every front page and TV screen: The New Reality. And not one person objected.

302

I would say more like how many of the liberties we were hoping to achieve got nipped in the bud and forgotten about. This thing is more about stopping people from escaping the clutches of being an employee than anything else that I can detect. It *might* be a dry run to see how we could cope with a really nasty virus next time. It's certainly not a concerted response to a genuine threat. My personal bet is it is part of a war on people being able to work for themselves rather than for their employer's benefit. Take one example, I know from the uncountable numbers of interviews and job offers I've had during the last few years, that nearly everyone requests WFH now. Every worker with kids wants it, every commuter wants it… people want that even more than better pay. So, they will leave their office job for any position where they can WFH. Employers (big business money controllers) know this. They ask themselves, how can we let people have WFH, without losing their loyalty and also not enabling them to lie in bed and do nothing all day long? This is a controlled exercise in testing WFH but also under the condition that "we're all doing this together" rather than "fuck you all I'm alright!" (which is the usual attitude of the few favorites who were hitherto allowed WFH). More manipulation, more enslavement… and this experiment can be called off if the controllers decide, on balance, "Nah, we need everyone back at work" and so put out via TV news "The virus has gone away, you have to return to your offices now!"

303

My last day at Thrombosis Research Institute (TRI) was today. Because we employees are WFH, I got a text (on Microsoft Teams) from the building caretaker, who's a mate, how's it going, sorry not to see you on your last day, etc. I joked back hold your horses, I don't know if it is my last day yet! In truth, I never was provided a confirmed termination-of-contract date in writing, and since I was given my notice by word of mouth last month, the whole coronavirus thing happened, the changes to the laws on freelancing that were the reason for my contract being ended were repealed, and because I'm still hard at work on projects, I had asked the bosses (via e-mail) to have my contracted extended, if only for a week or two. The caretaker must have conferred something about me to HR, because a few minutes later I received a text from them: "We hear that you are not aware that this is your last day. We cannot understand this, because you were clearly told that March 31st is your last day." I wrote back yes I remember but since then things have changed, including the reason you gave me to end my contract, and because I can't see any possibility of finding another job any time soon and I'm still busy here, I asked for a bit of help. The answer: "We do not know why you are not aware your last day is today." Then, I didn't hear any farewell message from any of the top management, not a word of thanks for my services, all day, nothing.

I'll be all right. It's scary being out of work but think—have I ever missed a meal? No. Have I been thrown out on the street? No. I've got Natasha and I prayed for her, isn't that the miracle I pleaded for? I won't forget that ever.

304

"When this is all over" (is the term):

1) I will be the only person who expressed doubt about the existence of this so-called virus—at least as an immediate danger to the community
2) I know that the overblown reaction is part of a big hoax
3) I realized straight away the underlying forces provoking the hoax are the same as in all previous, similar largescale hoaxes—protection of the rich and perpetual enslavement of everyone else
4) I have not joined in once in any single mass-hysterical reaction
5) I have not altered any of my behaviors through fear
6) I have openly told everyone what I think about this hoax—always at risk of what happens to anyone who stands up against the frightened masses—when they refuse to believe you and are prepared to fight you

305

"Capitalism once worked by conferring widespread deprivation. Now, it is being achieved by reducing to a false lowliness everyone's standard of what is desirable."—John Berger

"Divide and rule."—Napoleon

306

First, no one has, or has seen, or knows anyone with covid-19—that is, by direct experience. All the "famous" cases are merely TV reports—and may as well be among the "thousands affected" [news media insert any large number here]. Second, all the visual signs around us—the depleted supermarket shelves, the empty streets, the few stragglers outdoors in their surgical masks, the closed pubs, and so on—are themselves an end product of the hoax, not caused by the virus but by the hoax itself. It might look like covid-19 has decimated the population, but it hasn't—everyone is safely boarded up at home. Quietly dissenting voices by people I would always find more credible than TV news reporters, such as doctors, advise differently to the mass mainstream. I have heard doctors say that this virus is much less dangerous than the seasonal flu outbreak, against which there is never any reaction beyond elderly people and some other vulnerable groups are offered annual vaccines. I have also heard doctors attest they are being pressured in hospitals (by insurers) to diagnose unconfirmed patients with covid-19 and ascribe any mortalities they can to covid-19 on the death certificate.

When people are made to take steps *en masse* that are disproportionate to what might happen should no steps be taken, it warns me that these measures are for nefarious reasons. And those reasons are usually to my mind tied up with "How does the 0.1% of the world's population who own 95% of all the wealth manage to keep it that way?" The main means to do that is to keep the masses scared, worried, distracted. And divisive. Make them want to out-do, be suspicious of, and generally stay away from each other. Make neighbors not talk to each other, people at work not know each other, make everything a competition where "Our kids can go to a better school than theirs." Make this underlie everything—and they will never get together and start a revolt. And thus the very rich can keep their vast wealth. A (naturally occurring) viral outbreak blown out of all proportion is the kind of thing, like "threat of terrorism," that could be on a list of occurrences to exaggerate and escalate to keep the masses scared and divided—but remain working for companies owned by the rich. Need I go on? It seems that the Establishment requires something as big as this hoax perpetrated every decade, or maybe once per generation, so that the people carry their scars for life.

307

I had a timely dream last night. Background was before I went to sleep, my brother Chris in States said something about "nine hundred thousand cases of coronavirus and forty-five thousand fatalities so far." I said where did you get those numbers? TV? They're just numbers. They sound big so you believe them. But where did they come from? You don't know. They were promulgated on TV. As is, everywhere, declaration of "the new reality." It is slipped subconsciously into every news report—how we are coping with "new reality." It is in every news item, always slipped in imperceptibly—just to get under your skin. That alone makes me more suspicious than everything else. I said to Chris, if I were a magician pulling card tricks, I would insist that my magic were reality, right? So why does TV keep repeating the coronavirus is "reality"? It sounds very desperate to me—the insistence of a trickster.

Anyway, that texting conversation was followed later by my dream! I was in a big factory-like organization. It was (but wasn't—dreams!) Sankyo, large pharmaceutical company I first worked in Tokyo, back in the Nineties. I got a text, "Dr So-and-So" wanted to see me. I couldn't remember his name or where in this large factory complex he was situated. So I set off in search, haphazard. At one point I entered, several stories above ground level, a large warehouse. At the far end was the warehouse door, and I thought the place that I was seeking must be that way. To get down to ground level, I started to descend a rudimentary metal ladderway. After a few steps, it became simply a handrail with no steps. I considered to slide down, then realized I was stuck. Couldn't go farther down, nor back up. Two friends (Japanese) I recognized from my old soccer team walked past below, so I waved hi! This confirmed that I was indeed at Sankyo. Standing next to me all of a sudden were two workers, one man and one woman, wearing the boiler-suits that everyone donned at Sankyo. Without saying anything, they looked at me in a very characteristic Japanese way, which is nine tenths blank facial expression and just one tenth "So what are you going to do now (to get back up)?" The woman then, defying all gravity, held the platform level with one arm, and rolled upwards back onto the platform. The man's turn was next. Looking at me to follow suit, his ascent back up to the platform was even more wonderful— holding on with one hand, he backward somersaulted *à la* circus acrobat up and onto the platform. Neither of them said a word but the implication was "That's how you get back up." The platform was at my face level, and I had one arm on it and the other held a rope that was hanging down. With no idea what to do, and scared of the fall below, I tried / somehow expected to winch myself up in an impossible way—and then I awoke.

This dream showed me that magic, if it exists, is strange and incomprehensible, like defying gravity. If you show me a card trick, on the other hand, or "reality" as projected on TV, where they try to make it seem realistic but I have doubts, then I know it is a hoax. People will always try to fool you with illusions of "reality," but actual magic is not what you would expect to see at all.

308

[The coronavirus "epidemic" / hoax] is somewhere along the lines of what I've been saying since the start [February–March 2020]. It's an opportunity for the world's controllers to shepherd us, *en masse*, the world (the world's workers), into something that is of no benefit to us, but only to them. I've postulated that it is a response to the increased freedom that the internet has been allowing people to use their talent to make money for themselves rather than being someone else, some rich person's, wage slave. It's certainly to do with that, to my mind. And planned, along the lines of "We need the next viral outbreak, which we can predict will happen, because they occur in nature frequently enough, to instigate the new demographics we are planning." I've never said coronavirus doesn't exist. However, it is being used as a pretext to instigate changes that have been waiting in the wings for a while, is my certainty.

309

Here's another consideration when "all this is over." I never once stepped out anyone's way, cowered, or walked down the middle of the road out of fear of contact with people on the sidewalk. I don't believe that I'm at risk of infection and I don't encourage others to think that either. I'll state for the record. There could well be a virus going around. I have no way to disprove that. I have not seen or heard of anyone I know who has been infected or got sick. I am not worried about contracting it nor going outdoors. From the scientific literature I have read it is as unlikely for any individual to catch this virus from being proximal to anyone not displaying symptoms, even if a carrier, as (for example) it is to contract HIV by being near someone with that virus. The scientists who garnered an understanding of that by rational thinking back in the '80s and '90s went on to defeat HIV, fearful as that deadly disease was at first. Panic over coronavirus is beneath the intellect of human beings, akin to superstition about magical curses.

I write this because the spineless jellyfish who obey all these "new rules" about "social distancing" have betrayed our liberties—to go about our own neighborhoods—without uttering a word of inquisitiveness as to why, really, are we being brainwashed to do this? Some adult male just now saw me standing here typing this and nervously veered out into the middle of the road to walk past without getting too close. Chickenshit.

310

You can tell that the covid-19 hoax was dreamed into existence by businessmen and politicians without the collusion of medical professionals, whom you might normally expect to take a leading role in managing containment of a biohazardous outbreak, because it bears all the unsubtle hallmarks of heavy-handed philistines (e.g. strident news headlines, inconsistency) and none of the refinement of learned men and women. Moreover, the hoax lacks important principles enshrined in medical practice. Apart from all aspects of openness, one missing facet is informed patient consent. As a supposed infectious vector (human being) I was not asked whether I want to stay "locked down" at home, lose my job, or line up outside my local store waiting for "basic provisions." I was told to. Another ethical consideration ignored by the coronavirus hoaxers is patient confidentiality. People's medical conditions are supposed to be kept a private matter between them and their physician alone. Now everyone is publicly deemed contagious regardless of how they feel, and treated like Typhoid Mary. Designed to prey on fussy and over-cosseted people's nascent neuroses about germs and hygiene and washing their hands, the hoaxers concentrated their focus on the invisibility of microbial pathogens so as to terrify the public into a state of paranoia about uncleanliness and pestilence. Job done well done by the businessmen and their obedient puppy-dogs, the journalists in the news media.

311

If the powers-that-be, the very rich, from their hilltop fortified compounds look downwards and regard us poor people as a caste of untouchables and vermin that spread disease, and hence devise a "new reality" where we are ordered to wear hospital outpatients' rubber gloves and masks, isolate from friends and family, and wait in long lines for bread, then it's really up to us whether we want to play along.

312

Why did the controlling dominators who propagated this New Reality Apartheid call it "social distancing"? If it were a genuine healthcare stance, then why not borrow terms from medical practitioners trained to handle disease outbreaks, such as "infection control" "contact precautions" "managed care" and so on? "Social distancing" suggests personal isolation. "Social" means community, people, friendship, family. A mate of mine was not allowed to attend a love-one's funeral the other day. The deceased's send-off—the culmination of that person's life— was carried out remotely on a video monitor.

313

Waking Early Sunday Morning

The above title is a poem by Robert Lowell. Thought it goes well with the attached pic of Kew Green. There are a few people out now but no one to be seen when I got up at 6! Waking early Sunday morning. I write because when I walked past St. Anne's church and nodded towards Gainsborough's cenotaph, I realized the quiet sound of music I could hear was coming from an exerciser's stereo. This struck me how silent was the church this Sunday morning, closed down. Of all the many crimes committed by the people-hoaxers this year, probably the least noticed of all is the closed churches—places of quiet and refuges of spiritual power for those atuned. I couldn't care less about news but I care enormously about my life, and for once what's in the news impinges my life—this hoax. Someone owes me six months of my life they stole.

314

Shall we define hoax as a trick played on people unbidden to fool them into accepting something that is untrue. A hoax can be played for any number of reasons such as for fun but also, and always, to coax those persons duped by it to respond in ways that they would not otherwise, had they known the truth. The aim of hoax is to take advantage. It follows that hoaxers are in the know that it's a hoax, whereas the victims of the hoax are not in the know. And because a hoax was deemed the appropriate strategy required to persuade the hoaxed into reacting as calculated, rather than simply asking them to respond that way voluntarily, the victims must be compelled to do something they'd rather not. Now, since the so-called coronavirus pandemic is being masterminded by unknown people behind TV screens, for mysterious reasons and aims, which affect my life without consulting me or seeking my permission, then it is a hoax and I am one of its intended victims. This thing has been conducted by persons who abuse everyone's trust in news media and covid-19 is a hoax.